"For a generation that has not had great role models of what godly men look like, Brian's clarion call to live out the five marks of biblical manhood inspires and challenges men to be all God intended so that future generations have men worth following."

John Burke, *New York Times* bestselling author of *Imagine Heaven* and *No Perfect People Allowed*

"As a dad of four (including two teenage boys), I believe it has never been harder to raise young men. We have certain expectations of how our boys should grow into manhood, but they get many conflicting signals from the world around them and can easily feel that no matter what they do they can't ever measure up. Brian's insights into the marks of a man are spot on. They challenge me to my core, but nothing great comes easy. I find myself going back to these marks when I am making tough decisions or when my boy impulses might direct me in a way that is contrary to what God would want me to do. The marks are simple, easy to remember, and important, and we need to incorporate them into our lives so that we can be the *men* God intended us to be."

Kirk Perry, president, Brand Solutions, Google

"Contrary to what lots of folks seem to think, adolescence doesn't turn a boy into a man. A real man is far more than a boy with a few years under his belt. Thankfully, in this era of great confusion over what it actually means to be a full-fledged man, Brian Tome has written a helpful, timely, and at times hilarious book. I highly recommend it. You'll find it well worth your time."

Larry Osborne, author and pastor, North Coast Church

THE
FIVE
MARKS
OF A
MAN

THE FIVE MARKS
OF A
MAN

FINDING YOUR PATH
TO COURAGEOUS MANHOOD

BRIAN TOME

BakerBooks

a division of Baker Publishing Group
Grand Rapids, Michigan

Published by Baker Books
a division of Baker Publishing Group
PO Box 6287, Grand Rapids, MI 49516-6287
www.bakerbooks.com

Printed in the United States of America

Library of Congress Cataloging-in-Publication Data
Names: Tome, Brian, author.
Title: The five marks of a man : finding your path to courageous manhood / Brian Tome.
Description: Grand Rapids, MI : Baker Books a division of Baker Publishing Group, [2018]
Identifiers: LCCN 2018014308 | ISBN 9780801093708 (pbk.)
Subjects: LCSH: Christian men—Conduct of life. | Christian men—Religious life.
Classification: LCC BV4528.2 .T66 2018 | DDC 248.8/42—dc23
LC record available at https://lccn.loc.gov/2018014308

23   24   8   7   6

Contents

Contents

Acknowledgments

All truth in this book stems from . . .

The great men who have gone before me and built into me: Dick Tome, Denny Pattyn, Dan Lacich, Gil Hopkins

The men who journey with me: Darin Yates, Kyle Ranson, Art Schlemmer, Rob Seddon, Steve Smith, Judd Watkins, Mike Croci, Craig Dockery, Brian Wells, Jim Bechtold, Tom Shepherd, Glen Schneiders, Mark Stecher, Kirk Perry, Jerry Rushing, Chuck Mingo

The women who refine me: Kathy Beechem, Vivienne Bechtold, Usha Sklena, Susannah Croci, Dani Watkins, Michelle Smith, Molly Lindner

The wife who completes me: Libby Tome

The kids who bring me joy: Lena Tome, Jake Tome, Moriah Tome

How to Read This Book

If you would actually read a section in a book called "How to Read This Book," then you are someone who likes to read. If this is you, turn the page and start reading.

This book is laid out for the average guy, even though the average guy doesn't read this many words. Most guys don't read anything unless it is mandated for work. This isn't a judgment, just an observable fact. If they do read, it is in short bursts with the finish line in sight—think magazine articles, blogs, and book summaries.

If books this size intimidate you, simply read the introduction and the first chapter in each of the five marks. These brief chapters will give you the macro content. If you want to dig deeper, go through the rest of the book.

I believe every sentence and every chapter in this book has value, and I'm thankful for your trust as you give your time to grow as a man.

Brian Tome

Introduction

BOYS TO MEN

Once upon a time, a prince asked a beautiful princess, "Will you marry me?" The princess said, "No." And so the prince lived happily ever after and rode his Harley and four wheelers and had shotguns and poker nights and Call of Duty marathons and drank Pappy Van Winkle and smoked cigars *in the house* without a woman objecting and spent all his money on himself and lived every day like he was Ferris Bueller, while scratching himself whenever he wanted and leaving the toilet seat up.

The end.

Very funny and very true . . . if you're a boy. Don't get me wrong, I ride motorcycles, enjoy bourbon and tobacco, and leave the seat up (which my wife appreciates more than when I pee with the seat down).

I don't have issues with the vices mentioned. I have issues with the males I know who glorify these things and believe they are signs of their manhood. I know a guy who fits the bill but can't hold down a job to keep bills in his wallet. I know another guy who is so captured by the above lifestyle that he doesn't know how to capture the heart of a woman. These are males, but they aren't men.

There are fifteen-year-old men, and there are forty-five-year-old boys. Yes, you can be an adult boy, and you can be a teenage man. I've met many of each.

I have come to believe that the transition from boyhood to manhood is not marked by age; it's marked by things that are much more substantial, such as your mindset and your actions, assuming responsibility for your place in the world, and stepping into a new reality—one defined by strength, purpose, and a code of honor.

What is the cost of the absence of real men in our culture? Almost 33 percent of children in America are living in homes without the presence of their biological father. Children in female-headed families are four times more likely to live in poverty, repeat a grade, have emotional problems, struggle with depression, and be obese. The one thing that most prison inmates share in common is not race, age, or socioeconomic background; it's the absence of a father in the home.[1]

In an interview, writer and documentarian Sebastian Junger said: "I think this is probably the first society in history that actively discourages an intelligent conversation about what manhood should require of men. . . . Simultaneously, our society is asking adult males to be men." When asked, "But what's a man, anyway?" Junger replied, "[Society should] help define it. So that I can achieve it. So that I can know when I've crossed the finish line."[2]

My answer to the great question Junger was asked is outlined in this book. But the solution to the problem of absent men is not just a bunch of males reading this book and changing the way they do things. That would be great, but I believe, at its root, there is a deeper spiritual problem, and answering the question "What's a man, anyway?" needs to be approached with that in mind.

Studies (and countless news stories) consistently reveal that an absence of responsible, strong men is one of the most destructive forces in our world, across every continent. We desperately need our boys to become men. We males need a form of manliness that gets outside the paradigm of morality. This book isn't about glorifying Patrón tequila nor perfect attendance at church. If a man-eating lion showed up at your church, it would likely die of starvation, but this hasn't always been the case.

On April 15, 1554, the church was in upheaval. Various clergy members were questioning some of the standard practices in the church and wondering whether they should continue in their vocation. They questioned the indulgences. Why were they raising money for buildings by telling people that if they gave money, they could buy their loved ones out of purgatory? They asked why the church never discussed grace and faith. It seemed to them that the Church was losing its plotline. And then, even crazier still, they asked if they should allow people to read the Bible for themselves, rather than listen exclusively to what the professional clergy told them.

Hugh Latimer, who was seventy-five years old, said, "Let's make the Bible available in English." The authorities didn't like this at all. He was tried for his actions and sentenced to burn at the stake. As he walked to his execution with a younger associate named Ridley, he was overheard saying, "Play the man, Master Ridley, for we shall this day light such a candle in England as I trust by God's grace shall never be put out."[3]

"Play the man." Not "be a spiritually mature person" but "play the man." Being a man is a high and spiritual calling that needs to be reclaimed.

I've learned over the years that there's a relatively simple and ancient code that reveals what it takes to become a man. As you read, you will find that every man you respect holds to this code. Unfortunately, our culture has hidden that code under layers of enlightenment and progressivism, and it has doomed many males to perpetual boyhood. I don't want you to be just another boy victim. That's why I wrote this book.

And if you are already a man, you probably need some encouragement to keep doing what you're doing, because I know the world won't give it to you. Hopefully, you'll find it here.

On the day my son was born, I looked down on him in wonder. I leaned over and gently took hold of his hand with my thumb and forefinger. He proceeded to send a stream of urine up my arm that trickled down to my wrist. While cute in the moment, I knew it could be an omen of things to come.

My son, Jake, had soiled me, but that innocent act was nothing compared to how I had offended my own father. As a teenager, I gave my dad fits with my childish behavior. Fortunately, he was unaware of many of the things I did behind his back—getting drunk with friends, skipping school, smashing mailboxes with a baseball bat, using girls for my own gratification and sullying their reputations in the process.

As I matured and learned about manhood, I came to understand that those immature acts were just foolish attempts to prove my strength and masculinity. I needed to show myself and my friends that I was a man. In reality, those acts only proved my *lack* of manhood.

As I look back now, I realize that I was actually nothing more than a boy in a man's body well into my twenties. I wanted my son's trajectory to be different from mine, so I became a student of manhood. What I learned was revolutionary, and it changed my life.

In the traditions of nearly every ancient culture (and some modern tribal cultures), there existed a rite of passage that marked a young male's transition from boyhood to manhood. It was a public event that was deeply personal and declared to everyone, especially the young male, that from that day forward, he was a man and would enjoy the privileges and bear the responsibilities of manhood.

The specific content of the ceremony didn't matter. What mattered was that there *was* a ceremony—a defining event that was unmistakable and marked the passage from boyhood to manhood. In some cultures, boys had to climb a mountain and bring back an eagle feather. In other tribes, boys had to drink the blood of the first deer they killed.

I never had a moment in my life when I was declared a man. Because I didn't, I felt I had to prove my manhood in whatever way our selfish, "if it feels good do it" culture told me. I determined that my son was going to have a different experience.

He wasn't going to have to prove he was a man to the boys at a frat party. Instead, he was going to be called into manhood in an unmistakable way long before he encountered those temptations. (I'll share more about Jake's rite of passage later.) But to do that effectively, I had to be able to articulate exactly what he was being called into—what did it mean to be a man?

One day, as I was reading the book of 1 Corinthians in the New Testament, a passage jumped out at me: "Be watchful, stand firm in the faith, *act like men*, be strong. Let all that you do be done in love" (16:13–14 ESV emphasis added).

In this verse, to "act like men" was an honorable and aspirational statement. For many people in our culture, being a "man" means anything but that. Most adult males in pop culture are portrayed as buffoons. Every sitcom dad is just a slight variation of stupid Homer Simpson, Neanderthal Al Bundy, or spineless Phil Dunphy.

Notice that the text doesn't say, "Act like an adult" or "Act like a well-rounded individual." No, it says, "Act like men." It treats being a man as an ideal to be exalted and attained.

I did a mental survey of the men in my life I aspired (and aspire) to be like. Though they all had different experiences and professions, different personalities and upbringings, every single one of them exhibited the five marks spelled out in the verses above. When I saw these marks for the first time—the five marks of manhood—things started to come into focus.

1. Be watchful. I began to see that *men have a vision.*
2. Stand firm. What does this mean? It means that men aren't afraid to stand against the tide when they are resolved in what they believe. *Men take a minority position.*
3. Act like men. Notice that this command is written in the plural. I realized that this isn't just an individual journey. *Men are team players.*
4. Be strong. Men understand that they are wired to produce value. This means that *men work.*
5. Let all that you do be done in love. Things that are done in love are done for the sake of other people. This means that *men are protectors.*

These five marks form a code that defines what it means to be a man. A fifteen-year-old who exhibits the marks regularly is more of a man than a forty-five-year-old who doesn't.

Another verse in 1 Corinthians says, "When I was child, I spoke like a child, I thought like a child, I reasoned like a child. When I became a man, I gave up childish ways" (13:11 ESV). One way to paraphrase this verse is "When I was a boy, I spoke like a boy, I thought like a boy, I reasoned like a boy. But when I became a man, I gave up my boyish ways."

It's time for men in our culture to give up their boyish ways.

It's time for you to give up your boyish ways.

It's time to set a new standard for what manhood should be or, actually, to live up to the ancient standard that has been lost. No matter where you are in your life, no matter what you've done, you can choose today to be a man.

You can embrace these five marks and begin a new path of strength and integrity. Like so many of your brothers before you, you can choose to give up your boyish ways and become all that God has wired you to be.

It's time to man up.

MARK I

MEN HAVE A VISION

1

Boys Are Shortsighted.
Men Play the Long Game.

When I was a boy, I had one simple goal: an easy day. That's why I didn't want the academic rigors of college and why, when I finally decided to go to college, I didn't actually go to class. It's also why I racked up a terrible amount of credit card debt in my early twenties. It is also why I stayed in a predictable job for too long.

It took me *seven* years to finish my four-year degree. I took Accounting 1 three times. If I woke up on the morning of a final and didn't feel like going to class, I wouldn't, which meant I'd have to take the course all over again the following year. This was the downside of having my parents fully fund my education. I took advantage of their generosity. I was a boy who had no skin in the game, so I didn't care about the consequences of my behavior.

I didn't have a vision then for how an education could open doors for me. I didn't have a vision for how the discipline formed by simply showing up to class would teach me how to show up in the rest of my life. I didn't have the ability to project forward that an education meant more money, which could fund more meaningful pursuits. I didn't have a vision for saving money to fund something of lasting value in the future, instead of things that would quickly go out of style.

The book of Proverbs says, "Where there is no vision, the people perish" (29:18 KJV). Boys live only for today. They wait for inspiration to strike or for someone to hand them their big break or for the perfect woman to walk through the door. Men dream of something bigger, define it, and then work toward it.

Somewhere along the way, I began to see the power of vision. That's when I started to get manly. I decided to start working toward something significant, something bigger than what I was currently experiencing, something bigger than me.

At twenty-two, I had a vision for what a great marriage could look like, and I committed to Libby that I would work toward that, for better or worse, no matter how hard it might get.

At twenty-five, my first amazing daughter was born. Lib and I had a vision for what an authentic family could look like. Even though we were very imperfect people, we committed to sacrifice for each other and our kids in big and small ways to build a familial team that would stand the test of time.

At thirty, Lib and I were working full bore on the vision to start a church (Crossroads) for people who had given up on church but hadn't necessarily given up on God.

And we all lived happily ever after. Well, not quite. The decades since I first envisioned these amazing things have been an unpredictable, sometimes excruciating mix of wins and losses, wind sprints and exhaustion, and celebration and grief.

Don't get me wrong. This isn't a completed mission. I'm not done. *We're* not done. We're still in the middle of a struggle, and some days I get my posterior handed to me on a platter. It's not all pretty but there are periodic payoffs, and I'm thankful for every one of them.

One of the more significant rewards I experienced recently was my oldest daughter's wedding; she is the first of any of my kids to marry. Walking her down the aisle and giving her away was traumatic. I rarely cry but on that day the tears flowed. Then came the father-daughter dance. It was to the song—brace yourself for cheese—"Butterfly Kisses." That old song might make a red-blooded man roll his eyes. But you tuck your six-year-old daughter into bed and give her butterfly kisses and a memory is welded to the frontal cortex. I have that picture of us dancing framed and displayed in a place that ensures regular reflection on the mission.

I'm still working on my vision in an endless series of small daily choices, with a big dose of God's grace and a slew of awesome people around me. But I can tell you that even though I'm still in the middle of the journey, I'm in a season in which I'm tasting some of the sweet fruit of having a vision bigger than me on the long walk toward it:

- Lib and I just celebrated our thirtieth wedding anniversary on a camping trip with some of our closest friends. This incredible woman continues to make me a better man every day.
- My kids don't just love me, they like spending time with me. We would all say that our most fulfilling recreational and relational times happen with each other.
- The church vision we shared with a handful of dreamer friends when I was thirty has spiraled out of control (in a good way, mostly) to over thirty thousand revolutionaries going hard after God's work in the world, resulting in, among other things, eleven traditional Crossroads sites across two states and pockets of online attendees in forty-two other states sharing God's love with our neighbors. We've seen the establishment of the CityLink Center, which helps the working poor in Cincinnati and has become a model for work

around the country; six aftercare homes in India, which care for girls rescued from sex trafficking; and the largest privately funded AIDS hospice in South Africa (which later failed and was one of those posterior moments).

If you had told my twenty-one-year-old self that I'd get to experience all these things and more, I'd have thought you were nuts. Me? Undisciplined, "been in school long enough to be a doctor" me? No way.

However, when you begin to understand and experience the blessing that comes from stepping into manhood, it changes you. And God often gives you a vision that seems far beyond your present capability.

Sounds good, right? It is. But here's the fine print: it's hard. Get ready for resistance.

Our world loves big dreamers. Steve Jobs declared Apple's goal was to "put a dent in the universe."[1] Young Theo Epstein had the audacity to dream of breaking the World Series championship drought for the Boston Red Sox. And then did it. Twice. And then again for the Cubs. Elon Musk dreamed of electric cars, private space travel, and hyperloops.

These mad geniuses got headlines and high fives all around. Our world loves big dreamers. Great! So, what's the problem? The problem is our world loves big dreamers *from a distance*. Up close and personal, not so much.

The same crowds who applaud those big, audacious goals can often be the same people who are quick to bring you down to earth when you share your own big vision. This seems especially the case in religious circles. For some strange reason, it's considered a virtue to keep your dreams small and manageable.

Like a crab crawling up the wall of a pot, big dreamers quickly find themselves getting pulled back down by the other crabs. If that's been your experience, don't listen to the voices that assume if you're going after a big or bold vision, then it *must* be about you. But do remember that just because something is wrapped in spiritual language doesn't make it a God thing. So long as you are asking the question "Is this about me or about God?" then you are probably in a healthy place.

The world and too often Christians are cynical of success and big dreams. I don't know why this is because big dreams, big visions, and grand ambitions are sprinkled throughout the Bible. Consider Nehemiah. This manly man is an Old Testament hero who dreamed big and sought to rebuild the protective walls around Jerusalem. The walls used to be a source of national pride, but now they were indicative of their national disarray. In the midst of his attempt and eventual success, he was able to keep it about God and not himself. Yet there were critics who tried to get him off track or, specifically, off the wall. His detractors were distractors who attempted to get him to stop working toward the vision.

One day some boys called him out and accused him of not doing good work. He was working; they were criticizing. He was on the wall in sweat-stained clothes; they were on the ground in religious garments. He shouted down to them, "I am doing a great work and I cannot come down. Why should the work stop while I leave it and come down to you?" (Neh. 6:3 ESV).

In fact, the giver of dreams says the problem is actually the opposite: we don't dream big enough: "Now to him who is able to do *immeasurably more than all we ask or imagine*, according to his power that is at work within us" (Eph. 3:20, emphasis added).

I'm not talking about a self-serving dream so we can pound our chests as bigger, faster, or stronger. King of the Hill is a boy's game and the source of many of the problems in our world, not to mention some of the more annoying cocktail party conversations we'll ever get stuck in. If I've just met you and within five minutes we all know the Ivy League school you attended, your kid's SAT score, or the fact that you're a scratch golfer, you've got issues. I once heard comedian Brian Regan say he wishes he had been one of the early astronauts. Not for the adventure, but just so he could nip all those kinds of conversations in the bud with "That's great. I walked on the moon . . . after cruising in my looo-nar rover."

We're all susceptible to self-serving dreams. In pastor circles, we even find ways to wrap them up so they sound spiritual. "What's God doing in your church?" has often become a way for us to measure ourselves against one another. Sooner or later the attendance number question comes up, and someone ends up feeling like a winner and someone like a loser. (Specifically, *I* end up feeling like a winner or a loser. . . . I know, I have issues.)

As human beings, our motives in any endeavor will probably never be completely pure and altruistic. So what do we do? The answer is simple—but not easy. We keep going after big, God-sized visions and humbly walk with our God (Mic. 6:8).

There was a time in my life when I viewed every opportunity for advancement as a temptation to be selfish. It is easy to feel that way when only *other* people are getting bigger opportunities. If a friend relocated for greater responsibilities or opportunities, I felt abandoned. I was indignant that they couldn't be content where they were. Like Nehemiah's detractors, I tried to keep them from building a wall. The boy in me didn't want anyone leaving me for bigger things. In reality, I was threatened by their manly move for more. I was the crab trying to pull them back into the pot. When you have no vision, you don't understand people who do.

I had another shot at this scenario not too long ago. Kirk is a great friend and was a star performer at a local company. He had the opportunity to change companies and take a senior position with Google. My old boyish ways wanted him to stay put with me but the *man* inside of me knew not to listen to that old voice. Today, Kirk is a force inside of Google and in the Silicon Valley. He is a man with a vision who can impact culture in ways that

I can't, and now in a new position. He's an example of a godly man going after a vision.

Don't be afraid to dream big. What does that look like? How about launching a great company that puts a dent in the universe? How about turning the group of twelve-year-olds you coach into a band of solid young men? How about being the first person in your family to have a great marriage so that your great-grandkids can toast your love at your fiftieth wedding anniversary? How about buying some property in the country and building a log cabin with your own hands? How about all of the above? *Immeasurably more than all we ask or imagine.*

We can do this. It's not easy, but it's good. So let's get to work.

2

Boys Live for Today.
Men Think Long Term.

What is the last beer commercial that depicted a male with a vision? That would be . . . uh . . . none. Men are seen as perpetually adolescent boys who act like junior high kids or dirty old men.

Don't get me wrong. I know that losers like these exist. I actually know some of them. But there's another kind of guy who exists too. You just don't see him in beer commercials.

That being said, one of the greatest stories of vision I've ever heard is the story of a guy who actually *founded* a brewery. I read a book a number of years ago called *The Search for God and Guinness* about a man named Arthur Guinness who founded the brewery of the same name. Guinness noticed that older males around him were acting like boys. They were getting drunk and not taking care of their families because their only drinking option was Irish whiskey and hard alcohol.

He knew that getting men to abstain from alcohol altogether was a losing fight, and he didn't want to start a war he couldn't win. Instead, he decided to create an alcoholic drink that would allow someone to consume more ounces and not get drunk. Thus, Guinness beer was invented. He was a follower of Jesus who had a vision. The fascinating thing is he had a vision not only for the short term, one that some people would criticize him for, but also for how his family would be blessed by the business after his death.

He entered into a nine-thousand-year lease for his factory, for which he paid £100 up front. That's about $147 US. Then he agreed to pay £45, or about $66 US, a year for the remainder of the lease.

At the time, people must have said, "What are you doing signing a nine-thousand-year lease? That's a lot of money!" But Guinness had a long-term vision. In essence he said, "This gives me water rights for the beer and everything else."[1] He knew that he had to sacrifice in the short term to reap rewards in the long term. That factory is still standing and producing beer today. He's barely even a fraction into his nine thousand years. That $66 per year is looking pretty good.

That's what men do. Vision, by definition, requires us to break out of our short-term, overnight-delivery, instant-download mentality and engage in the long game.

In my favorite scene from the movie *Dead Poet's Society*, Robin Williams, playing a teacher at a private school, takes some students to a trophy case containing photos of former students. He tells them that the people in the photos are dead and rotting in the grave. They once were young and vibrant and now are food for worms. He then exhorts the boys to "seize the day" and not allow life to slip by.

I absolutely believe in seizing the day, but not in the way that most in our culture think. One of the ways to go from being a boy to being a man is to seize today and make your life extraordinary. But you do it for a big vision that's off in the future, not for the little, short-term buzz that many boys go after. YOLO! You only live once! That mantra is usually said just before partaking of boyish things like having another beer when you were good two beers ago.

To boys, *you only live once* means doing whatever is fun today. They're taking the path of least resistance, going after every amount of pleasure they can afford in the moment, rather than seizing the day for a vision of the future that will last.

Men, however, seize the day to work toward a vision. They know the work may be hard, but they also know that to reap the rewards they may have to defer immediate pleasure. I'm as much of an Amazon Prime fan as anyone. (The next time I plan to walk into an actual store, unless it's REI or a motorcycle shop, is exactly NEVER. Thank you, Jeff Bezos.) But the best things in life don't come with free overnight delivery. The interesting thing is that Amazon has built the most powerful retailing juggernaut ever by scratching our short-term, "want it now" itches through long-term vision. In fact, Bezos titled the opening section of his first shareholder letter in 1997, "It's All about the Long Term."

Amazon plays the long game like almost no one else, and it has been doing so for twenty years. First, we thought their game was all about being the world's largest bookstore. (Some investors mocked Amazon as a joke, convinced it was just an online bookseller wannabe that would get crushed by the big boys.) Then we thought it was the world's largest consumer goods retailer. Then the most efficient distribution pipeline ever. Then the largest-scale cloud computing service the world has ever seen. I'm not sure exactly what Bezos's final endgame is with all this, but apparently it involves me being able to get Alligator Beef Jerky delivered by a drone directly to my back door as God intended. That and revolutionizing how we read with the Kindle. Oh, and private space travel. (Beef jerky, drones, Kindles, and space travel. Game over. God bless America!)

As impressive as this is, there has been no greater nor longer-term vision in the history of the world than the one that the biblical figure Abraham was given. Abraham was happy with his comfortable and predictable life with the people and the places he had known his entire life. Enter God.

Now the LORD said to Abram, "Go from your country and your kindred and your father's house to the land that I will show you. And I will make of you a great nation, and I will bless you and make your name great, so that you will be a blessing. I will bless those who bless you, and him who dishonors you I will curse, and in you all the families of the earth shall be blessed." (Gen. 12:1–3 ESV)

Abraham is the first Jew, and he is now to have a vision to leave what he knows, to go to a place of greatness, a new nation that will be the center point of humanity. Abraham is also told to "'look toward heaven, and number the stars, if you are able to number them.' Then [God] said to him, 'So shall your offspring be'" (Gen. 15:5 ESV).

A whole nation from just him. Keep in mind that Abraham was a very old man by this time. And there were no little blue pills yet. But that's not a problem if you have a vision that goes on for generations. Here we are, thousands of years later, and nations have come and gone—but Israel stands. It is still the center of worldwide geopolitics. Who would have thought that this nation, which had been without a homeland, was nearly exterminated during WWII, then finally relocated to their original land, would still be relevant? Who? Abraham. And out of his seed came the one upon whom all world history would hinge.

There's no historian worth his salt who would disagree that Jesus was the most impactful man in the history of the world. I don't care if you're atheist, Buddhist, or something between, there's no question, Jesus is the most impactful because *he had and worked a vision*. And yet when he died, Jesus looked like a complete failure.

Think about it. He went to the cross and all the people who had followed him and his teachings abandoned him. They denied even knowing him! His closest friends were gone. He died alone, in the most public and humiliating way possible, next to common thieves. In the immediate sense, he died a loser.

But Jesus wasn't playing for the immediate. He wasn't playing for just his thirty-three years on earth. He had a long-term vision. He had in mind people like you and me, who would hear about him thousands of years later. He was doing what he had to do to connect you and me to God, and he knew he had to go through pain and loss in the short term so we could have something in the long term.

There is, however, a bit of a paradox when it comes to vision: vision is about the long term, but it needs to start *now*. At the risk of sounding like a cheesy motivational speaker (I promise, there'll be no walking on hot coals or tips for how to buy houses with no money down), there is no better time than now.

A movie producer friend of mine says that if you're creating an action movie, one of the things you must avoid at all costs is slow danger. Delaying danger and consequences is the death of a great adventure story every time. You can have a great premise, riveting characters, killer stunts, and special effects, but unless you have real and immediate stakes in the story, it doesn't work. *There's a bomb in the building and it's going to go off in seventeen days* doesn't keep you on the edge of your seat. Slow danger kills great stories. It also kills great lives. Unless we start now, our days will turn into weeks and weeks into months and months into years, and the next thing we know it's fifty years later and that awesome dream we had of becoming an astronaut or a big league pitcher is just something we talk about, like a vague memory from kindergarten.

At the Design School at Stanford University, there's a sign just outside the entrance of the main building that reads simply, "You Are Here." That is some deep truth. It's where we always have to start from—here.

I think one of the biggest lies the enemy circulates among men with a dream is that they're too young (tell that to Mark Zuckerberg or that little kid David with the sling) or too old (tell that to Ray Kroc, who was selling milk shake machines until at fifty-one he switched career paths; or Charles Flint, who founded IBM when he was sixty-one; or Abraham, who had a child and began a nation at an age when other guys just want to read the paper and gum their Cream of Wheat).

If you listen to the voices of those who don't understand dreams and visions that come to men of all ages, then your one shot at this life will not be well lived. The right time, the sweet spot, is right now.

You are here.

I met Gil Hopkins my first week in Cincinnati. Someone told me that he had a heart for innovative things that could reach people. When we met for lunch, I told him of the man, Denny Pattyn, who had brought me into a relationship with Jesus. Gil then told me, "I brought Denny to Christ." Sitting before me was the spiritual grandfather I never knew.

King David had his "mighty men" who always had his back as encouragers and physical protectors. Gil was that and much more to me and many others. Gil was a hardened cop who came to Christ later in life. He never had kids of his own, but there were scores of men in their twenties, thirties, and forties who considered him their spiritual father. As his knees and hips failed him and were replaced, he managed our facility by cruising around on a three-wheeled scooter with a gumball machine strapped to the handlebars. Kids came out of the woodwork to see him and get a piece of gum.

Some church people can be really mean. One guy got under my skin so badly that I didn't know what to do. I went to Gil because I knew he would somehow make the problem go away. And he did; I never saw the guy again. (A couple years later this same guy was rumored to have been seen on public access television, heckling a council member. It wasn't until then that I had confirmation

Gil hadn't whacked the guy.) I've never found anyone that could replace the role Gil had in my life.

Some of the men he invested in had the honor of ushering him out of this world at his funeral. If you have never seen a warrior carried out on their battle shield, you are missing something. Some people call it being a pallbearer, but that word is too mealymouthed and inaccurate to describe all the events surrounding the funeral for my friend and fellow warrior on the day of his burial.

Gil thought long term. He thought beyond the limits of his own life. At his memorial service, guys he'd impacted from multiple generations shared stories of how he had the right, tender word at the right time. Another talked about how Gil had swiftly kicked him in the rear when he was getting out of line or lagging too far back. Another shared the wording on a plaque that was on Gil's desk: "Life's journey is not to arrive at the grave safely, in a well-preserved body, but rather to skid in sideways, totally worn out, shouting 'Holy Crap, what a ride!'"

Paul, one of Jesus's early followers, wrote about the Gentiles, who were not a part of the nation of Israel and were considered spiritually immature. Paul warned early followers of Jesus not to emulate their immaturity:

> You must no longer live as the Gentiles do, in the futility of their thinking. They are darkened in their understanding and separated from the life of God because of the ignorance that is in them due to the hardening of their hearts. (Eph. 4:17–18)

In the vernacular of this book, we could substitute *boys* for Gentiles: "No longer live as the rest of the *boys* do."

Starting today, we think *long term*. Every day we work toward a vision by taking off our boyhood ways and putting on our manhood ways, by asking ourselves, "Am I going to be a *man* today or am I going to be a *boy*?"

3

Boys Drift.
Men Focus.

Next, we have to focus. Did you catch that while you were multitasking? I said, *"Focus."*

You might need to rewind and read that first line again if you were skimming while listening to a podcast, texting in your Chipotle order, and checking your fantasy football team. It's easier to multitask, half paying attention, than to home in on one thing at a time that will produce results.

Focus is hard. We are bombarded by the "attention economy," which is just some consultant's way of saying the world is screaming for our mind space and our wallets 24/7. The economy needs our diverted attention to keep the clicks coming, the ads playing, and the machine running. And so we give our minds to them in bite-size chunks—thirty seconds here, forty characters there, twenty-seven emails here. And we drift from one micromoment to the next. At the end of the day, when all the micromoments add up to twenty-four hours, we wonder how we got there. We simply said yes to whatever happened to come along. Classic boy stuff.

A man, though? A man with a vision knows the secret ingredient is focus. Focus is the bedrock of vision. Without it, vision is just a good idea. I can't tell you how many times someone has told me they have a good idea for a new business or a ministry or a movie. That's good. Good ideas are nice. Great ideas are even better. But here's the truth: ideas are only about 5 percent of the formula. The most important part isn't having the right idea; it's working the idea. Virtually any idea will do if you put your head down and keep running. Whether it's a strong marriage, a business that thrives, or a screenplay that actually gets produced, vision becomes reality through focus.

There's a classic scene in the old movie *City Slickers* when this old, gnarly cowboy, Curly, played by Jack Palance, tells Billy Crystal's character, Mitch, the secret of life. He says it's "one thing." You stick to that and the rest doesn't matter. (He actually said it in saltier cowboy language.) It's become known as Curly's law, and it seems to apply to everything from how you write great computer code to what you do with your life. What's your vision? Find it and focus. It's the way of the greats.

Bill Gates's early vision for Microsoft was simple and focused: a computer on every desk. He took a cue from Henry Ford, who wanted a car in the life of every working-class man. Simple *and* incredibly difficult. That's why they needed to be focused.

Steve Jobs said innovation was "saying no to 1,000 things."[1] He said he was as proud of the things Apple said no to as the things they said yes to. He took this same focus all the way down to everyday decisions such as what clothes he would wear. He had a set uniform of black mock turtleneck, blue jeans, and New Balance shoes that eliminated the need to spend valuable mind space on what to wear each day. It was the same for Einstein. Redundant dressing may be a bit extreme. (I have a lot of clothes, so I use other systems to retain space for focus.)

The point is, distracted and fragmented lives rarely make a difference. This is one of the reasons Google ate everybody's lunch in the search engine wars. They had a good idea and they delivered a great product, but they weren't the only ones with those things. They also had maniacal focus. I'm old enough to remember when Google was barely a noun, much less a verb. You didn't google something. You pulled up a search engine, Yahoo, AltaVista, Excite, Lycos, or a slew of others, which offered a million things on its home pages: news, sports, weather, local tips, stock quotes, classified ads, yellow pages (a relic from the days of phones that had cords—google it). In this sea of cluttered pages, who won? Google, with one box, two buttons. Focus. Today, $498 billion (give or take) worth of focus.

But focus isn't just a business lesson. It's a life lesson. Do you want to be a man of vision? You will need to focus. And to do that, you'll need to make some hard choices.

But focus can also make things more sustainable. During year two of Crossroads's life, I realized something needed to change. I was running at a pace that I couldn't sustain. My focus on starting and building a church was second to my focus on becoming more like Jesus and building a healthy family. But in all truth, Crossroads was getting more of my affection and time than my family and some days even Jesus.

So I started going away for six to eight weeks every summer to connect with my family and be a man outside my identity as a pastor. The snarky criticism I received was almost too much to take. I want to have a great work ethic, and I want people to think I have a great work ethic. Hearing someone incredulously say, "You are doing what?" or "Must be nice" accompanied by an eye roll was tough.

What many people don't understand is that this annual season of respite isn't due to a lack of attention span. It's a relentless focus on having a life of power for the long haul. Crossroads is now twenty-one years in, and I'm just as focused and motivated to build it bigger and deeper than I ever have been. Not only that, I'm also equipped to go about that task because I feel adequately rested. While other peers have burned out or tapped out due to moral failure or loss of focus, my heart is as healthy and motivated as ever. The key is focusing and making the right decisions.

Another word of warning. Consider this a public service announcement to men who want to make a difference. Men with vision. Men who focus. There are some rather unfortunate consequences to all of this: not everyone will like you. It's true.

Some will feel threatened because we're not focusing on *them*. If our focus is on something in the future, something here and now may not be getting done, and that makes people uncomfortable. Of course, if our vision doesn't include providing for and loving our family and serving others, then we need to revisit our vision. But once we're confident that our vision encompasses those things, we can say no to things that fall outside of it. Having a vision means asking ourselves each day, "Do I know why I'm saying yes to certain things today and no to other things, even good things?"

Gordon MacDonald's classic book, *Ordering Your Private World*, had a strong impact on me in this area. MacDonald points out the danger of not proactively seizing our time based on the priorities of what we feel called to do. He says that unseized time will be grabbed by dominant people in our world, who will do a better job at controlling our time than we do.[2] We don't want this; we need to seize our own time. Some people won't like this, but they need to get over it. We need to get over it.

If we get flack for disappointing people, we're in good company. For example, Jesus was completely focused, which resulted in many people being disappointed. Why would Jesus need to focus? He could do whatever he wanted, right? Heal the blind, multiply loaves and fish, bench-press a camel. (Okay, there's no record of that last one, but I wouldn't bet against it.) What's amazing is that when we read the record of his life and work in the Bible, we see a guy who had intense focus. He unapologetically said no to things that didn't fit his vision.

Luke told of crowds gathering and pressing near to Jesus with needs, but "Jesus often withdrew to lonely places and prayed" (Luke 5:16). Focus. Mark recorded an early morning when the disciples went looking for Jesus, who was by himself praying. They said, "Everyone is looking for you!" (Mark 1:37). Jesus basically responded, "Let's go somewhere else; I've got other things to do." Focus. There was even a time Jesus said no to a Gentile woman who begged him for help. He said to her: "I was sent only to the lost sheep of Israel" (Matt. 15:24). In other words, "Sorry, but I've got to focus on my fellow Jews right now." But she didn't give up. She pushed back and impressed him with her focus for *her* vision. So much, in fact, that he granted her request.

Another negative consequence of focus will be that some will think we're weird, abnormal. That's okay. Have you seen "normal" lately? We don't want that; we want to make a difference. We want marriages that can weather any storm. We want strong, mature, thriving kids. We want businesses built for the long haul.

Financial gurus say that between bloated mortgages, car loans, and credit card debt, the financial state for the average American family is broke. That's normal. If that's normal, we don't want it. We want to be abnormal. And that applies to much more than just money. If we want to be men with vision, we must be men with focus. Our ADD culture doesn't want this or understand it. "Normal" people would rather we remain distracted boys. It's easier for them to criticize than to change. We don't want that; we want to be different.

Focus.

4

Boys Look for Open Doors.
Men Break through Barriers.

Getting to work on December 3, 2005, was a bit more stressful than usual. It wasn't a stuck in traffic or nowhere to park kind of problem. This was an angry protesters kind of thing: angry protesters in front of our church, angry protesters ticked off at our church, angry protesters ticked off at *me*. This was the day we were dedicating our new auditorium and building expansion that cost tens of millions of dollars. I know that large building programs can be controversial, but I'd never seen this before. Something else was going on that I'll get to in a moment.

I thought the deal was start a church, help people, and folks will like you. I'm pretty sure I read that somewhere during seminary. And this wasn't the first time the protesters had shown up. They had been out there before. They had also written letters to the newspaper, given television interviews, and assembled an impressive triple threat of good old American firepower: lawyers, politicians, and bloggers.

Resistance is the refusal to accept something or an attempt to prevent something. To me it's always felt more like a poke in the eye with a sharp stick, a pit in my stomach, or, to go a little lower, a swift kick in the crotch.

I don't like it. I want things to go smoothly. It's not that I think everything has to go my way. I know we live in a broken world. Sometimes I hit on twelve and still bust. Sometimes it rains on my one day off. The world's not always a bowl of Graeter's Black Raspberry Chocolate Chip ice cream (google it, you're welcome). But when I'm doing the right thing, when I'm on a mission from God, shouldn't it be easier than this? In fact, *isn't conflict, resistance, and pain actually God telling me to do something else?* That's flat-out boy thinking.

Most of my educational history was one of regret. I had a bad attitude about school and bad study habits. I latched on to the lie that I just wasn't good at school. Actually, I was just too lazy to persevere through the homework. As a result, there were opportunities not open to me that were open to others with the same IQ but who had a higher perseverance quotient. They had a vision of their future that pushed them to persevere that I didn't have.

Boys look for the path of least resistance. They look for open doors and the instant gratification that can be found on the other side.

Everyone else is doing it. Why not me?

I think I'll take that easy job; that'll give me a lot of time off to hang with my friends.

Well, she didn't say no to sex so—open door! I'll just walk right through.

That's not vision. Vision for the future is *difficult*. Vision is about persisting in something that other people have given up on. A friend of mine reminds me regularly that "if it were easy, they would have sent a dog with a note." It's not easy to do things that have lasting value.

Our age has embraced a brand of spirituality that says if God is involved, it will happen without pain. Just trust him. No, it *won't*. That's a lie, a lie that boys tell each other to justify dreaming small and giving up early.

You don't see God opening doors for people and making things easy in the Bible. You see shipwrecks. You see failure. You see extreme resistance in the midst of years, decades, and even lifetimes of patience and labor. In fact, the New Testament says, "for a wide door for effective work has opened to me, and there are many adversaries" (1 Cor. 16:9 ESV). If you want an easy, open door from God, just know that there are likely to be adversaries, and this among other things will lead to suffering. Everything significant that will happen in your life will come through struggle and persistence. This is the paradigm for manliness we see in the Bible. Man after man is leaning into and pushing things forward. Men break through barriers.

One of my favorite men in the Bible is the apostle Paul. You might know him as St. Paul, Roman citizen, writer of much of the New Testament, inspiration for a certain German lager brought to you six frothy mugs at a time by a smiling barmaid.

Paul didn't know a lot about easy. Here's the advice he gave in a letter to his mentee, Timothy: "But you, keep your head in all situations, endure hardship, do the work of an evangelist, discharge all the duties of your ministry" (2 Tim. 4:5). "Keep your head," "endure hardship." Sounds more like something you do when doors are being slammed in your face than when they're opened wide. Here's what he says in another letter, this time to friends in Rome: "Not only so, but we also glory in our sufferings" (Rom. 5:3).

Glory in our sufferings? One translation says, "We rejoice in our sufferings" (ESV). What is this? Maybe we're misunderstanding him. Maybe he doesn't literally mean suffering. Is God some sort of spiritual sadomasochist? Part of what we see here is that God isn't relevant only for those who run vacation Bible schools.

He also has something to say to those of us who are in the school of hard knocks. He understands and is working in and through the difficult stuff we face. This shouldn't be written off as just a religious, motivational sound bite. It's helpful to get a little more perspective on what Paul is talking about. Here's a passage from another of his letters, this time to friends in Greece:

> I have worked much harder, been in prison more frequently, been flogged more severely, and been exposed to death again and again. Five times I received from the Jews the forty lashes minus one. Three times I was beaten with rods, once I was pelted with stones, three times I was shipwrecked, I spent a night and a day in the open sea, I have been constantly on the move. I have been in danger from rivers, in danger from bandits, in danger from my fellow Jews, in danger from Gentiles; in danger in the city, in danger in the country, in danger at sea; and in danger from false believers. I have labored and toiled and have often gone without sleep; I have known hunger and thirst and have often gone without food; I have been cold and naked. Besides everything else, I face daily the pressure of my concern for all the churches. (2 Cor. 11:23–28)

Imprisoned, flogged, exposed to death, lashed, beaten with rods, stoned, shipwrecked, in danger, sleepless, hungry, thirsty, cold, and naked. I don't know about you, but Paul wins when I compare our suffering résumés. I especially like the way he ends this list. He says in so many words, "And if that wasn't enough, I have to deal with church people."

So it's the beaten, flogged, stoned, shipwrecked guy that says to "rejoice in our sufferings." Why? Listen to his reason: "Because we know that suffering produces perseverance; perseverance, character; and character, hope" (Rom. 5:3–4).

Through our suffering God is building some very good things in us, things that take us beyond the ordinary, things such as perseverance, character, and hope. Things that are better than easy, comfortable open doors. The minority of American men have ever served in the military, yet most guys I know wish they had. Why? Because of the purpose and bonding that come from being linked with others in a struggle that is important and significant.

Good things cost us something. They just do. Vision is hard. It is laborious. Sometimes doors have to be knocked down. It is *intense*. It is fraught with uncertainty. When boys drop away because it's getting too hard, men keep standing, pushing, and laboring on behalf of their vision.

When I'm tempted to quit, I remember the times when I did quit and regretted it—for example, the time I quit following a budget and ended up in oppressive credit card debt. I also recall the times when I stuck it out and now enjoy the blessings, such as every day of my first year of marriage. Eventually, our biography contains a history of perseverance that will naturally carry us through hard times.

Hard times are a common theme through all great movies. My favorite movie is *Braveheart*. I'm actually fairly impressed that I've made it this far in a book about men without referencing it. It's closely followed by *Gladiator* and *The Patriot*. (If you haven't seen any of these, I give you permission to put this book down and go watch them. Maybe grab a bowl of black raspberry chocolate chip ice cream. Okay, then. Are you back? Good. And you're welcome.)

It's not that these are the only kind of movies I enjoy. (I've also been known to indulge in *Tommy Boy* or *Dumb and Dumber* if I'm in a more refined mood.) However, there's something about these warrior-against-the-world stories that move me like nothing else. Give me a story about an underdog and a righteous battle against all odds and I'm there, even if it involves guys wearing skirts (kilt, tunic, whatever; let's just call it what it is).

My friend who makes movies says it's because I'm connecting with "the hero's journey." You may have heard of it. It's this not-so-secret creative structure that underlies many of our favorite stories. From *Star Wars* to *Wolverine* to *The Walking Dead*, if you pull back the curtain you can see it in the skeleton of the story. You find a reluctant hero, a call to adventure, a series of tests and trials, an "all is lost" moment, and so on. And it doesn't work only for epic *Lord of the Rings*- and *Gladiator*-type sagas. You can also see its thumbprint in straight dramas, comedies, and even a musical like *La La Land*. (Not that I would know. Or if I do know, it's only because I served my wife by watching it with her. Not that I enjoyed it for myself.)

Why does this work across so many different stories? I think it's because there's a secret behind the secret formula. I think we connect with the hero's journey across such a wide variety of stories because there's a real-life spiritual truth we're responding to, even if we don't realize it. That truth is we're not built for idle comfort. We were not created to drift through open doors. God is building something much more valuable in us.

Barriers. Suffering. Perseverance. Character. Hope.

We connect with these stories because that which is true in Scottish forests, Roman arenas, and Carolina battlefields is also true in Chicago boardrooms, Southern factories, and Silicon Valley start-ups. God is up to something and it has nothing to do with easy, open doors. God is building heroes.

I know three heroes. These heroes were responsible for the protestors that night in 2005 in front of our church. The crazy thing was that we weren't being protested for developing a large, expensive building. We weren't being protested for taking some controversial, countercultural stand. We were being protested because of the money we were spending helping the poor.

Since the launch of our church in 1996, we've felt one of the jobs God has for us is to be part of the solution to poverty in our area.

As our church has grown, we've put more and more resources into bringing opportunity and hope to the working poor in our city.

The more prayer, time, and resources we spent on this, the more we saw the need for a larger vision than simply handing out clothes and food. The need was for a place that provided state-of-the-art job help, educational opportunities, skills building, financial education, barrier removal, and more all in one location, while also offering relationship and accountability. After much searching and praying, we found the right place.

An old slaughterhouse that had been empty for years is not a pretty thing. But there were three heroes, friends of mine, who saw something else. Mark, Tim, and Scott were men who saw the vision of what it could be—a place of hope. So we purchased it and began making plans.

And we all lived happily ever after. Well, again, not quite. But this is such a good thing. What could possibly go wrong? Who could resist a vision of turning an eyesore into a beautiful building? Who could resist something that would help the poor? And who could resist the strong arm of God, which would surely bring a speedy victory? That's what I thought. Cue the resistance.

As it turns out, there were some who had other plans for the neighborhood. They thought this project would lower property values and instigated a multiyear journey of angry letters, protests, legal battles, and political maneuverings. Through it all I watched these three steady, faithful men—a former business executive, a pastor, and a lawyer—stand up for the cause, take blow after blow, be ridiculed in public, and keep pushing through barriers.

It was a fight that took a lot out of them and time away from their families and other work. It was a fight that went all the way to the Ohio Supreme Court. But in October 2012, I stood next to Mark, Tim, Scott, and so many others who had worked tirelessly for nine years, and I saw the CityLink center open. It's a place that has in the last four years served over two thousand unique individuals, a place that other cities are now starting to replicate, a place of hope—hope that came from character that came from perseverance that came from suffering.

Boys just want things handed to them by their parents, the government, or someone else "out there." They expect their employer to give them automatic pay raises forever without earning them. Men accept that there are no free rides. When they are working a vision, they recognize that there will be cost and risk involved.

We have to do something *now* in order to get something *later*, which means forgoing temporary comfort. We spend less and save money now so we have it when we need it later. We go the extra mile on a project so that our manager sees how valuable our contribution is and eventually offers us new opportunities and responsibilities. When we are working a vision, we are thinking about the long-term payoff for our efforts.

You want your life to matter. I know you do. Every person whose life matters persevered through monotonous and difficult times. They even doubted their previous decision, themselves, or God. What they didn't do was quit.

Keep going. Hang on a little longer. You just may find that God meets you in the form of a breakthrough.

Perseverance. Character. Hope.

— — —

NOW DO SOMETHING

We both know life is much more about what we do than what we know. To help you move from the "knowing" zone into the "doing" zone, at the end of each mark of a man, I'll include some quick next steps.

Read about asking God for big things in Ephesians 3:20 in your Bible.

Questions to Consider

1. Do you have a long-term vision for your life? If so, what is it? If not, why not? Is it big enough or have you weenied out and downsized it?

2. How will you make decisions about what to say yes and no to today?

3. Are you doing things now that are difficult but are directed toward the realization of a future vision? What are they?

4. Do people around you know what you stand for and where you are headed? And are there people whose feathers get a bit ruffled because you draw lines? (That's a good thing!)

5. If you have an older son, does he know you believe he is a man? If not, how will you tell him? If you have a younger son, what are your plans to usher him into manhood?

And hey, if you were never declared a man by your father, and you are over eighteen, no worries. Here's your declaration: You are a man. Now go get after it.

MARK II

MEN TAKE A MINORITY POSITION

5

Boys Want to Go with the Flow.
Men Are Willing to Stand against the Tide.

I love water. I don't care if it's fly-fishing in Montana, water ski-ing in Tennessee, or scuba diving off the Florida Keys. I love all kinds of water, but my favorite is water with a little attitude. If you have ever launched a Jet Ski from a beach on Lake Michigan, you know what I'm talking about. To get out to open water, you first have to get past the break. It's not easy. You have to focus and take the waves straight on. You also have to be willing to get your face wave-slapped a few times. You must go against the flow to get where you want to be. But that's where the good stuff is.

And so it is with manhood. Boys always go with the flow. Men are willing to go against the tide when necessary.

Going against the flow is not easy. This reality might actually be the thread connecting each of the marks. While being a man can be incredibly rewarding and involve fun, adventure, and joy, it can be difficult. Such is the path from boyhood to manhood. It's hard, but it's worth it.

One of the things that makes this tougher than it need be is that we men of the twenty-first century are weenies. I know that's not easy to hear, but I think if we can admit it, we can do something about it.

One of my favorite books on the subject of manhood is *Manthropology*.[1] It talks about how modern men are not stretched physically by our culture and therefore don't have the same capabilities that were common in our forefathers. For example, consider the Roman emperor Nero and his army. They would go on long, physically strenuous campaigns. One of these marches would be comparable to two marathons a day for six days straight while carrying 60 percent of their body weight on their back. Today, the average guy gets winded carrying two grande lattes back from Starbucks.

Many of us have lost touch with what we're capable of because our lives, generally, are much more comfortable than the lives of our forefathers. *Manthropology* goes on to surmise that shin splints are an issue only in modern times because our bones aren't as hard as they used to be, given our cushy, soft-soled shoes. We are soft, literally. We've lost sight of what it means to push ourselves and to step out of our comfort zones, and not just physically. This is also true in terms of our mindset. It's easy to slip into a comfort zone and just go with the flow, and that's exactly what boys do.

I grew up in Pittsburgh as the steel industry was winding down. I knew my hometown as "The Steel City": a place where men worked in steel-toed boots and fire-retardant clothing, a place where every day you went to work clean and came home dirty, a place where you had to engage your muscles in order to get paid. It was a time and place when men were men.

These men wouldn't understand my physical ailments. In a little bit I'll have to get up from my Herman Miller Aeron chair and go to the bathroom. When I do that, I'll feel a tweak in my lower back. Turns out that sitting on your butt for a few hours and moving your fingers on a keyboard can be hard work.

I thought *I* was bad until my neighbor told me he pulled a groin muscle coaching his son's soccer team. That's right, he got injured coaching kindergarteners. He made a quick turn on the sidelines during a game and injured himself.

Men, we are slipping.

In the 1970s, a cultural movement began that placed a lot of pressure on women to conform to unrealistic standards of beauty. Many social scientists and psychologists have written about how *Cosmopolitan* magazine set a standard for women that is still today (unfortunately) being aspired to and followed. To be a woman in our society is a crushing burden. Magazines set a standard for how women should look, how their bodies should be shaped, how their makeup should be applied, how they should be able to balance everything in their lives—work, home, social life—and never break a sweat. This was (and is) an unfair load to place on women, and it causes a lot of pain.

Now the same thing is happening in men's magazines. The world keeps trying to get men to all be alike, think alike, and do alike, and there are all kinds of cultural cues telling us, "This is what a man does and what he looks like." The men in *Men's Health*, *Men's Fitness*, GQ, *Maxim*, and so on all look the same. The stories and features tell us the mark of a *true* man is how he looks, how he dresses, and what he buys. I promise you that, in previous generations, a man overly obsessed with how he looked was an outlier and a priss, but that's not so today.

You have to not only look hip but also do X, Y, and Z and own the most expensive gear and the latest toys. There are articles in those magazines about how to have a flirtatious office affair or how to have an extramarital affair or even how to play the field without getting burned.

Then there are manscaping, butt implants, calf implants, manicures, waxing, and pedicures. Listen, I'm not against people taking care of themselves, but I *am* saying we need to recognize that this is overobsessive madness and in no way defines whether we are real men.

Sadly, these things are becoming the expectation and in many ways are defining our cultural understanding of what it is to be a man. Most males spend hundreds or even thousands of dollars pursuing the standard set by TV shows and men's magazines. And boys, even grown-up ones, just go with the flow. They look for the majority opinion to inform how they should look, what they should think, and how they should behave. It's just too uncomfortable for a boy to swim against the tide. But unless you do, you will never get to the good places and be the man God created you to be.

Jesus says, "Enter through the narrow gate. For wide is the gate and broad is the road that leads to destruction, and many enter through it. But small is the gate and narrow the road that leads to life, and only a few find it" (Matt. 7:13–14). He's talking about having a great relationship with God and obtaining eternal life. And he's saying the majority of people are on the wide road that leads away from God and toward their own destruction. Why? Because it's an easier road! And it's where everybody else is. It's comfortable.

Why is the road that leads to life narrow? Because it doesn't need to be wide when only the minority is on it. The government gives money for highway projects because the roads need to be wide and smooth to accommodate the masses. If you want to be a man, you will not be on a well-maintained highway with everyone else. You will have a steep climb with few peers on a narrow and rarely traveled trail.

My favorite places to ride my motorcycle are off-road because these are the remotest places. There is no litter, no congestion, no signs of human life. They are also the most difficult places to ride because the trail is often narrow, steep, and rocky. But these kinds of trails lead to the most beautiful and rewarding places—places that are too difficult to reach for people who would rather polish their chrome than accumulate scratches.

The journey to manhood is a steep, uphill ascent in which you won't find the masses. It is the place where memories are created and character is formed. You are likely to accumulate scars, but these experiences make a man out of you. The marks signal to you and others that you are on a different path in a different journey in relationship with a God who is strong and resilient.

There's a passage in the Bible some refer to as "the roll call of faith." In Hebrews 11, the writer launches into a list of men (and at least one woman) who showed great faith such as Noah, Abraham, Joseph, Moses, David, and others. When you look closely at their stories, two things stand out: (1) they all placed their faith in a God who was bigger than they were, and (2) they all had to swim against the tide.

Putting himself at great risk, Joseph refused the temptations of his boss's wife and suffered for it. Moses stood up to the powers of Egypt and led an entire nation against the tide. Young David, with nothing more than a sling and a conviction to defend his people, stood up against the Philistine forces of war.

In fact, I think we would be hard-pressed to find a hero of our faith who didn't sometimes have to swim against the tide. Men, work on your stroke. Get in shape. Be a man who swims against the tide and goes the way of the greats who are remembered.

6

Boys Want to Fit In.
Men Aren't Afraid to Stand Out.

I used to tell my children stories when I tucked them into bed at night. One of their favorites is about a man who was in the minority going against the majority. The majority in the story was the nation of Israel. They were chosen by God and uniquely blessed, and yet time and again their leaders made terrible decisions because they wanted to be liked by the neighboring nations.

They wanted the same gods as neighboring nations. They wanted the same customs as neighboring nations. They felt weird and abnormal. It was uncomfortable.

So they broke God's commandments and altered their behavior in order to fit in. Occasionally, a minority voice, called a prophet, would spring up. These prophets represented God, but often they brought a message no one wanted to hear. King Ahab was one of those chasing after the majority and was far from God. The prophet who told him he was doing wrong was named Elijah.

The Bible says, "When Ahab saw Elijah, Ahab said to him, 'Is it you, you troubler of Israel?'" (1 Kings 18:17 ESV). You see? Ahab just wanted everything to be easy. "Stop troubling us! Let us do what we want and go along with mass public opinion and modern morality!"

The story continues with Elijah replying, "I have not troubled Israel, but you have, and your father's house, because you have abandoned the commandments of the LORD and have followed the Baals" (v. 18). The Baals were worshipers of a false god named Baal.

Ahab was a boy. You can be powerful and rich and still be a boy. He wanted to fit in. When Elijah brought him a minority report, it was troubling. "Are you the troubler of Israel?" he asked. Men in the minority *trouble* the majority. When a man stands up and says, "We shouldn't fudge our numbers just to hit quarterly earnings," others are bothered by it. When a man stands up and says, "You should treat your date better," it's not received very well.

As I put the final touches on this manuscript, movie producer Harvey Weinstein is in the news for sexually harassing and abusing women in order to have his way. It's amazing how many actors and directors are saying, "This is awful; I never knew." Yeah, right. You never knew that you were so blind and weak. There's no question Weinstein exhibited his true colors in conversations with other men. There's no question guys heard the rumors. But none of these boys wanted to speak up.

Elijah would have spoken up long before the media did. What he said to King Ahab wasn't popular, but he continued to boldly confront others: "Elijah came near to all the people and said, 'How long will you go limping between two different opinions? If the LORD is God, follow him; but if Baal, follow him.' And the people did not answer him a word" (v. 21).

Often, when the majority is faced with a challenge, they don't have the guts to admit it. The masses couldn't even answer this simple and direct question. They were too comfortable to be bothered.

I have found that the events that most marked my life were those times when I was in the minority. We tend not to remember the times we're in the majority, because they're not all that special. The moments that define us as men are when we choose to do something that's difficult that we know won't be a popular choice.

One of the first manly moves I made was when I was fifteen or sixteen and received Christ in my life. I became Jesus's follower, and his Spirit entered me. I realized that doing my normal thing on Friday and Saturday nights needed to change. I could no longer go out and get wasted with my friends.

At the same time, people said to me, "Hey, now that you're a Christian, you need to get away from those people." They were telling me to get in a holy huddle with a lot of people who I thought listened to bad music, to only hang out with them. That's not the right thing to do. God doesn't want us to abandon friends when we come into a relationship with him. He wants us to stay in those friendships so that he can work through us to bring them into a heavenly relationship with him.

What did I do? I kept going to parties, but I realized I couldn't go and just stand there. I had to have something to drink, but I didn't want beer. So I took my red Solo cup and filled it with—apple juice. I was able to hang out and laugh with them. Some people asked, "Hey, what are you drinking?" They got really bummed when I told them, but it didn't matter. Regardless of what they thought, I was doing what I knew was right, even if I was in the minority.

I look back at other things I've done, even as a parent with my son, to which the majority responded, "You shouldn't do that." I felt it was important to bestow trust on my son and let him use things others were afraid to let their sons use. My son was five when I bought him his first slingshot. It wasn't a wimpy cardboard thing with a cotton wad on it. It was one of those powerful types that went over your forearm. It seemed that whenever I went out of town, I brought him another sharp object. He had an entire knife collection, and believe it or not, he never stabbed himself or hurt anyone else. People said, "You're training him up in violence. It's dangerous." I felt I was bestowing a trust, and I was okay being in a minority position, even though others were upset with me.

As I mentioned earlier, our church started a center in Cincinnati called CityLink, and it's awesome. It helps people break the cycle of generational poverty. Now, everyone loves it, but it wasn't always that way. When the project first began, there were picketers outside the building, negative editorials containing bad information, and people who, though initially supportive, jumped ship when the tide of public opinion turned.

Why is it so gratifying now to see everyone come alongside us in this endeavor? Because we acted like men. We said, "We understand this isn't popular, that we're in the minority, but we're going to stay the course because we believe this is right." Now that CityLink is open and helping so many people, the majority is in full support. It's great when you can be in the majority, *but never aspire to be in the majority. Never allow the majority to dictate your beliefs and your actions.*

Winston Churchill is attributed as saying, "You have enemies? Good. That means that you've stood up for something some time in your life." But boys don't want enemies. They don't want anyone to dislike them. They want to be invited to all the parties. The moments in my life that I'm most disappointed about now are when I had a transcendent, primal awareness of what needed to be done but failed to take a minority position or take the counsel of the minority.

One of the worst seasons of my life was when a person in leadership at something I was heading up had authority that didn't match their character. This person was divisive and built walls between people by sowing seeds of distrust. Their MO was to get people to fear others and believe that this person was protecting them. What is disturbing to me is not just that I didn't see it but that I ignored counsel from those who did and who said something wasn't right with this person. I ignored those who took a minority position and spoke truth. As a result, there was eventual carnage. Waiting for a bad situation to resolve itself rather than handling it right away always results in more pain.

I still sometimes avoid accurate, albeit negative, warnings from those in the minority. I still have boyish moments. It's a lifelong battle that all of us who aspire to manhood have to fight, but the more experience we have in taking a minority position, the more familiar and easier it becomes.

Let's return to Elijah for a moment. When we left the story, he had just called out the Baal worshipers. Then he said, in so many words, "Here's what we're going to do. We're going to see whose god is real: the god of the majority, Baal, or the God of the minority, my God, the ancient God of Israel. We'll each take an animal and put it on an altar. You'll pray to your god and see if he answers by sending fire to devour the animal, and then I'll pray to my God. Whichever god answers with fire, that's the real God. Deal?"

And everyone said, "Deal." The Baal worshipers went first.

> And they took the bull that was given them, and they prepared it and called upon the name of Baal from morning until noon, saying, "O Baal, answer us!" But there was no voice, and no one answered. And they limped around the altar that they had made. And at noon Elijah mocked them, saying, "Cry aloud, for he is a god. Either he is musing, or he is relieving himself, or he is on a journey, or perhaps he is asleep and must be awakened." (1 Kings 18:26–27 ESV)

Elijah said, "Dudes, it's not working. Where is your god?" He even said, "Maybe he's relieving himself. Maybe he's stuck on the porcelain throne and he's got a really good scroll that he wants to get through before he comes." He's totally jabbing at these guys.

He's totally trash-talking them. So the prophets of Baal amped up their intensity and started chanting louder and louder, ripping their clothes to get their god's attention, and cutting themselves, and blood started to flow.

I loved telling this story to my kids when I tucked them in at night. Little kids love hearing their dad talk about bowel functions coupled with a Bible story. They also loved the dramatic voices of the different characters and the sound effects of the climactic moments. At this point in the story I said, "Nothing happens. [long pause] *They give up.*"

Then it was Elijah's turn.

Elijah the prophet came near and said, "O LORD, God of Abraham, Isaac, and Israel, let it be known this day that you are God in Israel, and that I am your servant, and that I have done all these things at your word. Answer me, O LORD, answer me, that this people may know that you, O LORD, are God, and that you have turned their hearts back." Then the fire of the LORD fell and consumed the burnt offering and the wood and the stones and the dust, and licked up the water that was in the trench. And when all the people saw it, they fell on their faces and said, "The LORD, he is God; the LORD, he is God." And Elijah said to them, "Seize the prophets of Baal; let not one of them escape." And they seized them. And Elijah brought them down to the brook Kishon and slaughtered them there. (1 Kings 18:36–40 ESV)

What a scene. The prophets of Baal fail. Elijah says, "Bring the bull. Put it right here. And while you're at it, bring me some water too."

Water? Water and fire don't mix. Water beats fire. They bring water up and they dump it on the bull. They get another barrelful and dump that too. They keep doing it until the trench around the altar that's meant to catch the blood of the animal is completely filled with water. Then Elijah says this simple prayer: "Let them know that you are God." At this point, I created a lightning storm with my mouth and spewed saliva all over their sheets. I explained, "Fire comes down from heaven, burns up the sacrifice, burns up the altar, evaporates the water instantaneously. [long pause] And *that's* our God!"

And just like that, the nation of Israel got down on their hands and knees and said, "This is the true God." The majority came to see that the minority was right.

Recently, I came across an article about a man named August Landmesser.[1] He was a shipbuilder in Nazi Germany. There is a famous photo of him at a ship dedication in which everyone is doing the salute to Hitler.

Everyone except *him*.

The majority of Germans in 1936 thought they were doing the right thing by going along with the Nazi agenda. The majority wins. This guy took a minority position and it cost him. He was arrested and eventually drafted. Nobody knows what happened to him. And why did he refuse, by the way? Because he had a Jewish wife. That dude was a *man*. That man was right, and that man was in the vast minority.

Guys, don't think about the huge challenge that you might face in the future. Think about whatever it is right now that's on your heart in which you are in the minority and need to stand strong. History will likely show that you were right and the boys were wrong.

Take a minority position in the little things so that when a big thing comes along, you've developed the muscles you need to meet it head-on.

7

Boys Are Fractions.
Men Are Whole.

It's quite amazing that I'm writing a book, given my history with education. My fourth-grade teacher nearly crushed any desire I had to learn and engage in scholarly pursuits. I'll call her "Mrs. Smith." I learned later that she had a reputation for not having patience with nor liking boys, and boy, did I experience that. I know I was no angel, but I was also regularly intimidated and made to feel inferior and stupid. As a result, I lost confidence and rebelled against the idea of school.

One thing I do remember from that year was what an integer is. It is a whole number, any whole number, not a fraction or a decimal. Integer is where we get the word *integrity*. To be a person of integrity means to be a person of wholeness, a person who isn't fractured, a person who is consistent at all times and in all situations.

There is a major integrity crisis among men in our country. Guys have gotten used to being different people in different places.

Most think nothing of having different language standards at the office than they do in front of their kids. Many professionals nod their head in agreement when the Bible says, "Thou shalt not lie." Yet when they have given their word to someone on a business agreement but later learn there may be a better deal elsewhere or they could squeeze the person for more, they renege on their commitment and say something to the effect of, "It's just business."

Every time I've heard that phrase, it has been in the context of someone trying to justify their lack of integrity. When our words don't line up with the contract, then we aren't whole. We are operating only in fractions of the truth instead of being people who are wholly true through and through.

The reason for every loss of integrity is because someone didn't want to lose: didn't want to lose the commission, didn't want to lose the quota given the quarterly earnings, didn't want to lose a little larger payday. It is one thing to hate to lose. It is another to forfeit a piece of your honor in order to get something more.

Later on, you will learn a little about Man Camp. It is a two-day adventure at which men stretch themselves physically, spiritually, and relationally. At the opening orientation we say, "Your vices are welcome here. If you have a cigar on your deck at home, you can have one here. If you have a Jack and Diet at home, you can have it here. If you drink beer, we have sixty kegs here for you."

Some would say only persons who don't have integrity drink and use tobacco. Those same people tend to see the world through moral glasses marked "right" or "wrong." I know this may surprise some of you, but the Bible never says, "Thou shalt not smoke." Nor does it say, "Thou shalt not do anything that is unhealthy."

Now, I don't think it is a good idea to smoke two packs of cigarettes a day. I don't think God wants us to abuse the bodies he has blessed us with. But I also know that two cigarettes a day isn't any less healthy than the food choices the average American makes every day. I also know that if you harbor bitterness and unforgiveness, medically speaking you are doing the same damage to your body as you would with two packs a day. Interesting how the bitter moralists see Jesus clearly telling us to love, pray for, and forgive our enemies and yet refuse to love, pray, and forgive and don't realize they have lost their integrity.

Have you ever noticed that when a guy is alcohol free, tobacco free, fat free, gluten free, caffeine free, sugar free, and fun free he tends to not have a rich relational life? Some sociologists theorize that the reason for their loneliness is that other men don't feel safe around him. They wonder if he is hiding something or clinging too tightly to his life or operating in fear. They wonder if he would put his life in danger for the welfare of the group. This is why most men have a guttural reaction of suspicion toward someone who has no vices.[1]

To be clear, some of the most courageous people I know don't drink, don't chew, don't smoke, and don't date girls who do. My good friend Brian Wells has none of my vices, and I know he would jump on a grenade at a moment's notice for me and anyone else in the room. Yet I had an almost instinctive wariness about him when we first met.

Men, don't take up a vice if you don't have it now. If you've been fine up to this point, there is probably no good reason to start. You don't need a vice to be a man. But I will tell you this . . . stop clinging so tightly to your life. The thing that makes us desire safe choices is the same thing that causes us to make unhealthy compromises. It is the fear of losing something—the job, a bonus, or our lives.

Jesus tells us to pick up our cross and follow him. A cross was a means of execution. Jesus wasn't asking us to wear a piece of jewelry shaped as a cross or a shirt with a cross on it. He was telling us to be people of integrity and to be like him through and through. We should be so wholly one with him that we would be willing to lose our lives to follow him. We should be so ready to lose our lives for the right reasons that we metaphorically carry around a means of execution (the cross).

When I was in seminary, I had a class that required a certain amount of theological reading. At the time, I had a new baby and a job, and I was overwhelmed. I procrastinated, and as the semester drew to a close, I realized there was no way I was going to be able to log the required hours. So I did what a person without integrity would naturally do. I fudged the report. I lied about reading books and chapters that I hadn't.

I did get a good grade in the class and felt good about it. But as the next semester began, I didn't feel right. My conscience wasn't whole because I knew I had fractured my integrity through that lie. As the semester progressed, I couldn't put my lapse out of my mind. The only way to make it right was to go to my professor and confess. I knew that this violation could cause me to be kicked out of school. My mind tried to convince me otherwise: *God has forgiven you and you know he wants you in ministry. Why confess and risk ruining his plan for your life?*

Though he doesn't share my vices, Brian Wells and I have a lot in common. One of which is we hate yard work. We don't fertilize, we don't aerate, and we couldn't tell a tall fescue from a zoysia (I had to look that one up). But I do keep the grass cut and the weeds pulled. (Or at least someone in my family does. Full disclosure: it might sometimes be my wife. There, I said it. I'm a man and my wife sometimes cuts the grass.) So where was I? Yes. Brian Wells.

He would cut his grass only when he absolutely had to and forget about edging or mulching or anything else in your typical homeowner's lawn arsenal. He was even less of a lawn guy than I am. He had a quote from author Sloan Wilson in his study that read, "A man who wants time to read and write must let the grass grow long." Brian thought it was funny.

His wife didn't.

After years of being in their old house, he came out one day to a disturbing discovery. Just outside the front door, his porch was crumbling. Upon closer inspection, he discovered that the weeds he had left untended had grown up around the base, multiplied, and were now actually eroding the concrete foundation of his porch. What used to be tiny little weeds were now doing great damage. That's not a hard picture to make a parable of:

Small weeds + Time = Big problems

Men know that this isn't a story about lawn care; it's about life. It's about the little things. It's about this thing called integrity. Boys tend to think life is all about the big moments. What would we do if we had to lie to save someone's life? Or if a bag of money fell off the Brinks truck and no one was looking? Or if, when minding our own business walking home from school, a group of supermodels drove by and kidnapped us for a weekend in Vegas? (Was I the only one that worried about that potential character test when I was younger?)

When boys think about integrity—being men of their word, honorable business partners, trustworthy friends, faithful husbands—they think it's only about doing the right thing in the big moment.

It's not that big tests don't come. But more often than not, they are an accumulation of a lot of little tests, of many little choices that add up. Probably the biggest scandal of my lifetime has been the one involving President Richard Nixon and Watergate. (You know a scandal is big when its name becomes part of the name of every other scandal that comes after it: Contragate, Spygate, Deflategate.)

I was very young at the time so I don't have an actual memory of it, but we all know the basics. What at first looked like a small-time burglary at the Democratic National Headquarters ended up leading all the way to the Nixon White House and a stream of lies and deception from the president and his top aides.

It brought down a sitting president and changed our country forever. In the years since it broke, one of the big themes that repeatedly comes up from many of the key players such as John Dean, Chuck Colson, and others is that it wasn't a single big incident that they compromised on. It was a slow drip, drip, drip of questionable choices that built up almost unnoticed over time within the core team. None of them woke up one morning and decided to betray the country's trust. It was a slow, steady pattern of small, almost negligible compromises, a slow killing of their consciences.

Back to seminary. I felt that something was being killed inside of me as I harbored and justified my actions. My conscience was dying. My relationship with God was dying. I realized I would rather lose a shot at my seminary degree than lose those things. So I went to the professor and confessed. Thankfully, he gave me grace. He offered forgiveness and no consequences. Wow. It was a blessing, and I learned a lot that day. I learned about second chances. I learned about how an older man can impact a younger man. And I learned that I was a person of integrity. I was whole, and being willing to lose something proved it.

While boys are fixated on the tests of the big moments, men know it's much more about the daily test of the trivial. It's our small, everyday choices that shape our character and prepare us for the big moments. As with many other aspects of being a man, integrity is not something we ever nail and can forget about. Small weeds never stop springing up. We won't ever get to the place where we can say, I've got this integrity thing down. I can cross that off the list. On to the next thing.

I've invented a motorcycle part that hundreds of people around the world have ordered and paid for. It's beautiful having a side business that has brought a lot of found money into my life. For the most part, this business operates under the radar with checks in the mail and other hard-to-trace money.

The government would never find out about it unless I disclosed it on my taxes, which is exactly what I will do. It has meant keeping records for the explicit purpose of giving the government money. I love my country, but I don't love paying taxes. I do it because it is a move of integrity. I could easily cut corners, but in doing so a weed would grow in my character that would erode my foundation.

Here's how Jesus described this to his disciples: "Whoever can be trusted with very little can also be trusted with much, and whoever is dishonest with very little will also be dishonest with much" (Luke 16:10).

Men, encourage God to trust you and give you responsibility. Show him that you are whole and not divided. Step out from all the weenie boys who may have success and a lot of accolades but who don't have the respect of those closest to them. Be willing to lose for the right cause.

And then go have a beer.

8

Boys Crave Independence.
Men Embrace Interdependence.

One of the greatest days of my life was when my oldest daughter got married. I'm not proud to say that I had been stressing about that day since the day she was born. Weddings are expensive, and I was never sure how I was going to pay the bill on a relatively meager salary in the midst of mortgages, utilities, food bills, education expenses, medical expenses, and on and on the list goes.

When Nick, my now son-in-law, asked my permission and then popped the question, I had to go into problem-solving mode for a day I wasn't fully financially prepared for. Through God's grace and the help of friends, money was not an issue. Friends stepped up to take care of food. Others handled parking; others took care of setting up and tearing down the facility. At the end of the day, I had one of the most rewarding days imaginable, and it was financially stress free. And it was because of my dependence on my wolf pack.

When necessary, men swim against the current. This, however, does not mean that we swim alone. We're not lone wolves.

One of the most destructive myths that has grown out of the last fifty or so years in the United States is that boys grow into men when they achieve independence. Not true. Like all good lies though, it has a piece of truth in it. But it's just that—a piece and not the whole thing. Is movement from dependence on others, particularly our parents, a key part of the journey from boy to man? Absolutely. Will it be a sad day when I'm old and need my kids to assist with bodily functions? For sure, especially for them.

But it doesn't stop there. Men realize there's another stage, an even more advanced stage, God has designed us for: interdependence. From the beginning of all that is, God has designed us to be interdependent. Men can't live and reproduce without women. Women can't live and reproduce without men. The sexes are interdependent on each other. Why is it this way? Maybe it is related to the triune God being interdependent—with himself.

This is a book for men, and it is a lot easier for me to talk about man stuff than deep theology. But we can't fully understand our need for interdependence if we don't see God as being interdependent. He exists as one in three separate persons: Father, Son, and Holy Spirit. They complement one another, they operate together, and they are one and interdependent on each other. If God has made man in his image, as the book of Genesis tells us, it is no wonder that things don't work out for us when we strive to be independent.

Interdependence is when we stand on our own two feet but make ourselves open to relationships. The best teams, the best work groups, the best circles of friends do not settle for independence; they push for interdependence. That's when we're so much more than the sum of our parts. That's iron sharpening iron (Prov. 27:17).

I'll talk a lot more about that in the section on the third mark of a man, but there's one specific aspect I'd like to cover here: decisions. Some of our toughest decisions will be exactly those times when we need to go against the crowd. How do we do that? Go with our guts? Follow our hearts? Pick another cheesy cliché?

The only way I've found to work through those kinds of decisions is by getting into the Bible, prayer, and community.

Remember Paul from chapter 5, the guy who dealt with shipwreck, beatings, imprisonment, and more—and kept going? Here's what he says about the role of Scripture in our lives: "All Scripture is God-breathed and is useful for teaching, rebuking, correcting and training in righteousness" (2 Tim. 3:16).

Every decision needs to be held up against Scripture. Sometimes the decision-making process stops right there. If I feel God is calling me to something that requires me to leave my wife and kids and fend for myself, I don't need to do a lot of soul-searching about it. God's already made it clear in the Bible that choice would be selfish and wrong. I am one with my wife, and I can't leave. That would be like willfully leaving one of my legs behind.

The danger here is that sometimes we can find a seemingly perfect but out of context sound bite from the Bible that supports what we want to do. Instead, we need to take into account the full picture God gives us in Scripture and then work to make the right application to our situation. There are many topical Bibles available, or you can google the topic on a Bible webpage. You will find a wide range of Scriptures that can indicate a true north heading.

The challenge, of course, is that for many of our decisions, the answers aren't always that clear. When the Bible says I need to work at whatever I do "with all [my] heart as working for the Lord, not for human masters" (Col. 3:23), it's clear I'm called to bring my A-game to my work. It doesn't say, however, whether I should be a carpenter, accountant, programmer, or something else. Fortunately, God doesn't give us just the Bible.

Elsewhere, Paul also writes: "Do not be anxious about anything, but in everything, by prayer and petition, with thanksgiving, present your requests to God. And the peace of God, which transcends all understanding, will guard your hearts and minds in Christ Jesus" (Phil. 4:6–7). Prayer. So what is prayer? It's simple, really.

Prayer is having an internal conversation with God in which we tell him what we're up against and ask him to give us direction. The trick is to not only talk but also listen. Even in the middle of crazy circumstances, we are to create some space to talk to God about our struggles and then be still and listen. And often he will speak. Not necessarily audibly; in fact, I've *never* had that happen. But what I have experienced is a realization that the Bible passage I had been looking at that I didn't think related to my situation actually did, and it became clear what it meant for my circumstances.

Most often though, I don't have clarity on the big things until I lean into the third leg of the decision stool: community. That shouldn't really come as a surprise. When you look at the story of how God has worked throughout history, his ways almost always involve groups, clans, bands of brothers (and sisters)—from the tribes of Israel to King David's mighty men to Jesus's disciples. It's a trend that we still find true today. Guys who make an impact never do it alone—Lewis and Clark, Hewlett and Packard, Phineas and Ferb. I could go on.

Groups that have affected me and altered the trajectory of my life have been countless small bands of brothers I've met with over coffee or beer for seasons of my life. They've been men who have given me the right word at the right time. This includes guys I lived with in college, staff members like Gil who were with me in the fight to build something great, or friends I ride bikes and camp with who have deep and sometimes difficult things to say to one another around a campfire. "Plans fail for lack of counsel, but with many advisers they succeed" (Prov. 15:22).

I've continually found these friendships to be the third leg in my decision-making stool, the counselors, the advisors that I need. I don't hang out with these guys simply because they're a great resource for decision-making; that's not how it works. We hang together because we're friends. (Okay, some of them have a lot of money and bless me with things I would never have otherwise. I may be able to be bought but I'm not cheap. But other than that, they're just my friends.)

Counsel from close friends is particularly important when we're wrestling with big decisions because it makes it tougher for us to succumb to what is called "confirmation bias." Confirmation bias is when our decisions are driven more by what we *want* to be true than what really is true. This bias is wishful thinking, and it's a classic sign of boy behavior. It's good for our short-term peace of mind and egos but bad for our long-term reality.

I've heard that one of the traits that makes a great investor is the time they spend looking for "disconfirming" information. Once they come up with a theory about the market value of a company and its future prospects, rather than devoting a lot of time to finding information that proves their theory is right, they spend a disproportionate amount of time looking for information that proves their theory is wrong (disconfirming information). Having done that, if their theory still looks solid, they invest. There's something about close friends who can help us see not only what we want to see when faced with a tough decision but also what we can't or don't want to see. "Wounds from a friend can be trusted, but an enemy multiplies kisses" (Prov. 27:6).

Years ago, at lunch with a friend, I was supposed to be having a good time eating bottomless Olive Garden soup and salad. At that point, my life was comfortable and predictable. I wasn't really stretched in my job. But I wasn't really thriving either. But that was okay; I had just enough money to pay an uncle a relatively low $350-a-month rent for a cute little house on an acre of land. I was set, and I wasn't going anywhere.

Then while munching breadsticks, Tom said to me, "I want to ask you a question. What are you doing here? I don't mean in this restaurant; I mean in this town and at this job. You have gifts and abilities that are not being used, and you need to put them into play somewhere else."

Ouch. It was complimentary but also very challenging. Tom took a minority position, and it was good for me. In fact, had he not said that a lot of lives would be different.

One of the things that separates men from boys is that men realize they won't grow from only hearing what they want to hear (or what is delivered in the way they want to hear it). Boys surround themselves with people who will tell them the things they want to hear. Men take advice and counsel from friends—even when it's tough to hear, even when they might not agree with it, whenever and however they can get it—because they know it makes them smarter, better, and stronger. "Like an earring of gold or an ornament of fine gold is the rebuke of a wise judge to a listening ear" (Prov. 25:12).

The thing that made my friends' gifts of serving at my daughter's wedding so sweet wasn't that it saved us a bunch of cash, although it did (thanks, guys!). It was that these were guys with whom I'd been through the not-so-great times—lost jobs, broken relationships, and sometimes the sharing of hard truths.

This is the kind of interdependence every man needs and a boy never experiences.

— — —

NOW DO SOMETHING

Read Jesus's words about narrow versus wide paths in Matthew 7:13–14.

Questions to Consider

1. Can you name a time recently when you took a minority position? How did it feel?
2. When faced with criticism, what is your default reaction? Does your default need to change?
3. Is there something in your life right now that you've softened your position on, or avoided altogether, because of the potential for criticism?
4. Who do you know who is currently taking a minority position? How can you give them your support?
5. What discipline can you build into your life to strengthen your ability to take a minority position and withstand criticism?

MARK III

MEN ARE
TEAM PLAYERS

9

Boys Are Lone Wolves.
Men Run in Packs.

We think lone wolves are dark, mysterious, and strong. They become the stuff of legends. The truth about lone wolves, however, which I learned from an animal trainer in the mountains of Montana who owns previously wild wolves, is that they are weak, malnourished, and have short lives. Wolves need a pack with which to circle and kill an animal. They need a pack to huddle with for warmth and protection. Lone wolves don't get enough to eat, and they die early and alone.

Lone wolves are losers. In the wild, lone wolves can't thrive, nor in life can men thrive on their own. We may be able to fund an early retirement on our own, but we can't truly experience and enjoy life without some brothers. Worse yet, we all have permanent or temporary weaknesses that a brother can help us navigate or even overcome.

If there was one spiritual discipline I could immediately give to you, what do you think it would be?

Some might say reading the Bible. Wrong.

Some might say prayer. Wrong again.

Some might say going to church. Still wrong (though you are always welcome at Crossroads).

Cynics might expect this megachurch pastor to say giving more money away. Wrong yet again.

If there was one discipline I could impart to every male, it would be this: *Choose the right friends, and leverage them wisely.*

Male friendship is a spiritual discipline, and it needs to be elevated. I will take someone who knows how to conduct a manly friendship over someone who is good at nearly any other skill. If we know how to maintain strong, godly friendships, we will make fewer mistakes in our lives, and we'll recover more quickly from those we do make.

This truth should impact not only our relationships with other men but also our relationships with women. Women feel vulnerable when they see the men in their lives on their own. Men are dangerous when they are lone wolves.

Being a lone wolf may be why males commit suicide at almost four times the rate of females and represent almost 80 percent of all suicides.[1] A leading theory is that female adolescents are encouraged to feel comfortable being in relationships and leaning into other females, whereas society tells young males that they need to "be strong and independent" and "man up" and "be your own man." They are not supposed to need anyone else in their lives. It's weak to need others. But the isolation eventually causes them to crash, and when they do, there is nowhere to turn.

In his book *Love and Survival: The Scientific Basis for the Healing Power of Intimacy*, Dr. Dean Ornish speaks to the importance of relationships: "I am not aware of any other factor in medicine—not diet, not smoking, not exercise, not stress, not genetics, not drugs, not surgery—that has greater impact on our quality of life, incidence of illness, and premature death from all causes."[2]

We will physically die earlier if we don't have great friends, and that will be after we have already died spiritually. In fact, if we don't have great friends, we are spiritually dead already. Someone may argue with me on that, but I've seen it too many times to be convinced otherwise.

I wrote earlier that taking a minority position is an important mark of a man. That doesn't mean doing everything on our own. It's a lot easier to take a minority position when we have real friends supporting us. Every great revolutionary in history had a group of friends to back them up and support them when things got rough. William Wilberforce had the Clapham Sect. Martin Luther King Jr. had the Southern Christian Leadership Conference. Nelson Mandela had the African National Congress. And lest we forget, Jesus had his twelve disciples (even if things didn't work out so well with one of them), and a core three—Peter, James, and John—he regularly went off with. Men are team players.

The most traumatic day of my life started with a phone call. I was greeted by the emotional and terrified voice of my oldest daughter, who blurted out, "Dad, Mom just had a stroke, and she is in the ambulance on the way to the hospital."

One of the hazards of the job of a pastor is that I hear of awful things happening to people more often than the average person. I not only know thousands more people than the average person, but I also get more prayer requests than the average person. People don't ask, "Hey, would you mind praying for me for wisdom with all the money God has blessed me with?" Instead, and understandably, the prayer requests are typically for medical emergencies and tragedies. As a result, I have a rolodex in my mind of all sorts of maladies and what naturally occurs with each one.

As I was preparing to leave the house to rush to the hospital, I scrolled through my mental rolodex for "stroke." The results were all negative: facial paralysis, permanent loss of speech, wheelchair, feeding tube, death. As I entered the hospital, I wondered if my days of having a conversation with Lib were over. I contemplated how I was going to do my paying job when my number one job was likely to become a primary caregiver.

As I entered the room where my wife lay, medical professionals were buzzing around and doing their jobs. My wife was looking at me without the ability to speak or move. The kids came in the room and we prayed fervently and awkwardly in front of a bunch of doctors and nurses who were looking blankly at us and who may not have understood what we were doing nor why we were doing it.

As they wheeled her into the operating room, we were left to pray, wait, and wonder what our family's future was going to look like. While we waited, one patient was wheeled out of another operating room in a body bag with family members following and weeping. It was an incredibly stressful morning, to put it lightly.

Finally, a nurse came out and brought us to the surgeon who filled us in. He said, "We went into the artery at her groin up through her heart, and I pulled out the clot in her brain and then squirted medicine in the area. She has blood flow again, and she is talking."

Relieved, I said, "So we are looking at a full recovery?"

The surgeon replied, "Let's not assume that right now. She is going to have some processing and sequencing issues. This is going to be a journey."

When we finally saw her in the intensive care unit, she could speak slowly and with a stutter. Normally, that would have freaked us out. But given that she could communicate and wasn't drooling and didn't have a feeding tube, I was ecstatic.

Throughout the morning my friends were calling and texting me with encouragement. They had all immediately left their day jobs and camped out in the parking lot of the hospital to be available to help in any way possible. I knew I had brother warriors who would move heaven and earth to make a difference. If I had said, "I'm really stressed right now and one small way you could help is by shutting up a guy at the church who's been bothering me for years," they would have done it. (By not asking my friends for favors, I may have saved some lives that day because I think they would have done anything to help me.)

As Lib was stabilizing under the care of the medical professionals, I was able to head out to meet my friends in the parking lot. I was greeted with hugs, prayers, comforting words, and the simple gift of their presence. They offered me my favorite beer. I don't normally drink at 11 a.m. on a weekday, and I have never drunk in a hospital parking lot, but it was a way for them to empathize and say, "We are thinking of you and want to give you a reprieve."

To make a long story short, my wife was a medical miracle. She walked the stairs inside of twenty-four hours of having the worst kind of stroke you can have. You aren't supposed to have all the blood cut off from half your brain for hours and still be able to walk out of the hospital forty-eight hours later and play tennis the following week. We are thankful for medical technology and for a God who still says yes to healing conditions medicine alone normally can't fix.

But this isn't a chapter about miracles and medicine. It is a chapter about friendship. The wife of one of those friends in the parking lot that day has a friend whose young child suffered a catastrophic illness. The woman and her divorced husband, the father of the child, sat together with their son for three days until he died.

For those three days, that man sat in relational isolation. There were no friends who came to support him, no brothers for him to lean on, no community to bring him a beer. I want better for you. I can't impact you and your family's medical future, but I can try to impact your friendship factor.

You and I need significant friends. If they are missing in your life, the time to fix that is now. Eventually, it will be a nonnegotiable need in your life.

10

Boys Are Passive. Men Are Active.

A couple decades ago, the book *Men Are from Mars, Women Are from Venus*, describing the differences between the sexes, was everyone's favorite book. It declared that women go to lunch, and men go to their cave.[1] It called out the fact that men are not good at friendship; they go off to be alone whenever possible. Unfortunately, this is largely true, but it shouldn't be.

It's also important to understand, however, that male friendships look different from female friendships, and they should. Male friendships are at their best when they have a few specific attributes. One of those attributes is that male friendships are *active*.

Why is there an unusual bond among guys who served in the military together? It's because these men were *doing* something together, and in the process a strong friendship was formed. Sebastian Junger has written extensively about bonding in his book *Tribe*,[2] and the principles contained therein are seen in his documentaries.

I once heard him recount a story of a returning Afghan war vet who was invited to speak to his hometown women's auxiliary group. At the close of his talk, one woman raised her hand and sheepishly asked, "Is there anything you miss about serving in Afghanistan?"

The soldier quietly reflected for a moment and then said, "Ma'am, I miss almost all of it."[3]

I don't think he missed the death, the blood, nor the sleepless nights in a foxhole. What I believe he was saying was that being engaged in an active mission with others did something for his soul that American civilization does not. Our culture with all its demands and electronic gizmos divides us; it doesn't unite us. On the other hand, when we find ourselves without our smartphones inside a foxhole with brothers, the friendship equation increases exponentially. We don't have to be in the military to have great friends, but we need to be engaged in something with other guys to have the possibility of true friendship.

I hope never to be in a military foxhole. However, I am in other kinds of foxholes right now, actively engaging with other guys, which results in deep friendships being formed. I have a lot of lowercase f "friends" whom I enjoy being around. I have fewer capital F "Friends" with whom I do life. The difference in the smaller group is that there is an activity that draws us together.

There are three dominant sectors in which I have significant friends: staff at Crossroads; young entrepreneurs, because that's who God is calling me to connect with right now; and adventure motorcycle riders.

These are activities I'm interested in and drawn to. If you are too, then we have mutual, natural playgrounds that we would both self-select in which we would experience the finer points of friendship: laughter, encouragement, counsel, and accountability.

Men building real friendships by actively doing something together is seen repeatedly in the Bible. One of the greatest stories of this type of friendship is the story of David and Jonathan. David was an amazing warrior and had amazing male friends, one of whom was Jonathan, also a great warrior. They both understood how to use weapons. Jonathan and his armor bearer wiped out many in battle all by themselves. David also slayed many enemies in battle. They bonded over this as fellow warriors.

Men who have real friendships develop them by finding areas of common interests. They find things they like to do or are good at (or can get good at) and take notice of who else is doing them. These are potential friends. Actively doing stuff with other guys who have similar interests is the breeding ground for male friendships. Many of us are void of relational connection because we haven't actively engaged with others since high school or college.

At my tenth high school reunion, there was still an amazing bond with people I hadn't talked to in a very long time. Why? We were guys who had battled on the gridiron (and a lot of other things that my publisher won't allow me to tell you about in this space). These activities acted as fertilizer to grow deep roots among us, and we were able to pick up where we left off at a moment's notice.

That bond didn't come about simply because we weren't married yet or had more free time. More discretionary time made spending time together a bit easier, but I think the core reason is because we were *doing* something together. Maybe it was the unique bond that comes from lining up next to each other in a three-point stance on Friday nights. Maybe for you it was robotics club or stage crew for the school theater. You didn't build those friendships by sitting around in a circle and talking about friendship; you did something—you competed, built something, served together—and friendship happened. Oxford professor and author C. S. Lewis, who had a deep friendship with J. R. R. Tolkien of *Lord of the Rings* fame, put it this way: "You will not find the warrior, the poet, the philosopher, or the Christian by staring in his eyes as if he were your mistress: better fight beside him, read with him, argue with him, pray with him."[4]

Beyond high school and college, developing close friendships doesn't happen as naturally. We have to make an effort. We have to

Boys Are Passive. Men Are Active.

make time for it and allocate money in the budget for "man stuff."
It's important. Most male friendships happen around activities.
But almost all of these activities cost money.

Risk is probably involved too. Young males in our country ages
eighteen to twenty-four are three times more likely to die than
young females.[5] Why? Because they take more risks. They are out
experimenting, trying things, and bonding. I remember as a kid
blowing up mailboxes with M80s. I can't believe I still have all
my fingers today. We made tree forts thirty feet in the air out of
scrap wood held together by a dozen reclaimed nails in branches
the size of my thumb. It's a miracle we survived.

During those times, deep friendships were born. But they likely
wouldn't have if we had just sat on the back deck and drank lem-
onade together. Nor would they today if the extent of the activity
was sitting in a coffee shop drinking coffee or in a bar drinking beer.

My son, Jake, and I have a deep relationship with one another.
It's a relationship not based on being father and son but one built
on adventure and difficulty. A couple months ago, we went on a
bike ride and our five-hundred-plus-pound motorcycles got stuck
in mud and loose rock. We worked for three hours to move them
ten yards to safety. We were totally spent yet wouldn't trade the
experience for anything. Our bond was deepened and strengthened.

Back to David and Jonathan. There's something about risk
and action that draws men together, and this equation was their
relational glue. After Jonathan's death, David wrote:

> I grieve for you, Jonathan my brother;
>> you were very dear to me;
> Your love for me was wonderful,
>> more wonderful than that of women. (2 Sam. 1:26)

Some people read this and think that David and Jonathan were
gay. The idea that our culture would see this verse and come to

that conclusion shows just how little our culture understands male friendships. Men are told that being close to other men is effeminate. *That's a lie.* Or if you love another man, you must be gay. *That's another lie.* Our culture has told men that we don't need anyone as long as we're strong enough. *Not true.* Men need other men to help them come alive and be strong.

By the way, I'm uncomfortable when men say that their wife is their best friend. My wife is not my best friend. That's too low a description of what she is. First, we are one flesh—not two people, one flesh. Second, there are things a guy can say to me that she can't. There are things a guy will inherently understand about me and my issues that she can't. We're just different. In my experience, when a man says his best friend is his wife, it probably means he doesn't have great male friends.

When I moved to Cincinnati, the first thing I did was find a place to play basketball. Why? Because I wanted to make some guy friends. One of the saddest days of my life was when I had to walk away from basketball because my back could no longer take the pounding.

Why was I bothered by this when I can still exercise in other ways? Not because I missed basketball, though I do miss the days of getting my teeth caught on the net (though always a little embarrassing). The reason I was bothered was that I knew when I left I would be leaving behind friendships. We try to get together once a year to reconnect, but it never goes much further than that because we aren't *doing* something together. Men, if you want to develop good friendships, center them around activity.

I originally worked on this chapter while on a plane to Arizona with five friends. My son trailered six bikes to Phoenix for us. I had just turned fifty and wanted to ride from the bottom of Arizona to the top of Arizona and around the Grand Canyon all on dirt and camping all the way. On day five Jake hit a rock so hard that his engine cracked and it began gushing oil. It was awful in the moment and gloriously awesome at the same time. It forced all of us to man up a long way away from civilization to figure out how to get him and his bike out. It was taxing, intense, expensive, and worth every sweat bead and every dime. I'm a rich man because of my friendships.

What are the sectors in which you build friendships? You don't need many, just one or two. I don't know what they are for you. One of my friends is into model railroading, and guys come over to build sets and talk about their hobby. Maybe for you it's knitting. That might sound a little unmanly, but you need to find whatever captures your imagination and enables you to connect with other guys of similar interests.

Male friendships are active.

11

Boys Reject Authority. Men Respect Authority.

Male friendships have *authority*.

I played tight end for the JV football team. Or at least that was my assigned position. I wasn't actually playing much because another guy was getting more snaps. He was older than me and not as good as I was. That is how I saw it. I assumed the best thing to do was to ask my coach in his office why I wasn't playing more. My heart wasn't to question his authority. It was simply to ask if he saw things in my game that were weak and needed improvement.

Unfortunately, the coach didn't take it that way. He reamed me up one side and down the other. It was loud enough that everyone outside the office could hear it. He continued his rant while we were on the field doing stretches. I'll never forget him pacing and saying loud enough for everyone to hear: "Football and coaching are not a democracy!"

He was right. And yet I was right too. There is nothing wrong with asking someone in authority an honest question. But I had to submit to his authority.

Yep, I said it: the "A" word. Some guys recoil at the word *authority*. Maybe they've seen it abused in the past. Maybe by a parent who was all about the rules but not so much about love or relationship. Or by a teacher they didn't connect with or a coach who belittled them. I get it. It happens. We've all experienced some abuse of authority. But I also know I wouldn't be half the man I am today without a handful of very impactful authority figures in my life, both past and present.

Authority is a lot like a Stallone movie. When it's good, it's great. When it's bad, it's terrible. (By the way, the last movie in the series isn't *Rocky 7*. It is called *Creed*, and it is moving, and you should see it.) I once heard someone say that one of the reasons pain in a marriage can be so intense is because the greater the potential for intimacy, the greater the potential for disappointment. I think that applies in some way to authority. When it's bad, it can be incredibly damaging. When it's good, it's powerful and life-changing. So just hang with me on this, because it can be good.

Most of us say we don't want any authority in our lives but our own, but rugged individualism is a recipe for disaster. It's the best way to remain weak. The absence or abuse of authority is one reason men remain boys. It's also why groups of boys often wreak havoc. Search through the scandalous stories of Enron, World-Com, Lehman Brothers, inner city gangs, and entitled frat boys, and you'll find boys running without authority. The same is true for an even longer laundry list of religious and political scandals.

Having no authority in your life is the best way to remain a boy. If you want to be a strong man and rich man in every way, you need to have authority in your life. It's one of the key ways you grow.

Just as lone wolves in the wild can teach us about the need for a pack, so too the story of male elephants in South Africa's national parks can teach us about the need for authority.

I've been to South Africa many times and have seen elephants in their national park system. It is well known that in the 1990s, officials at the Kruger National Park game reserve were faced with a growing elephant problem. The population of African elephants, once endangered, had grown larger than the park could sustain. Elephants eat a massive amount of vegetation and trample just as much. A high concentration of elephants can throw off an entire ecosystem and lead to the death of plant and animal species. Something needed to be done to thin the ranks.

This problem still exists, which is why "culling" or legalized hunting is such a controversial topic. Fortunately, they had another option. A plan was devised to relocate some of the elephants to the Pilanesberg National Park game reserve, which was underpopulated with the majestic beasts. Due to their enormous size, elephants are not easily transported. At the time, technology existed to transport only the smaller ones, not the larger and more mature bull elephants.

Sometime later, a strange problem surfaced at the younger elephants' new home. Rangers began finding the dead bodies of endangered white rhinoceroses. At first, poachers were suspected, but the huge rhinos had not died of gunshot wounds and their precious horns were left intact. The rhinos had been killed violently with deep puncture wounds. Not much in the wild can kill a rhino, so rangers set up hidden cameras throughout the park. They found that the younger elephants were killing the rhinos. This had never been seen before. It appeared to be part bullying, part vandalism, and part machismo.

The theory was that these younger males were wanting to mate but the females knew they weren't ready. Females will mate with only the largest and strongest bull elephants in order to strengthen the species. As a result, these sexually frustrated males vented on the rhinos. Two elephants seemed to be the ring leaders, so a hunter was authorized to kill them. But the problem continued. Other young males stepped into the void with the same behavior.

By the time the rangers figured out what was happening, technology had caught up to the point that they could bring in some larger male elephants. In 1998 full-grown bulls as old as forty years were transported. The largest, Amarula, was approached aggressively by one of the young bulls that had previously had his way. Amarula greeted him with a thrust to his stomach that lifted the younger bull feet off the ground.

Overnight, the problem went away and order was restored. There was no more senseless killing in the park because an authority was on the scene and in charge. The bizarre and violent behavior of the juvenile elephants stopped completely. Gus van Dyk, Pilanesberg's field ecologist, said, "I think everyone needs a role model, and these elephants . . . had no role model and no idea of what appropriate elephant behavior was."[1]

We too need role models who are authorities in our lives, not only serving as examples but also demanding that we toe the line. This is a high calling for men in our culture, and it is a source of strength that boys should be forced to recognize.

Authority takes different forms in a man's life. There is the formal relationship structure, a chain of command that many of us have in our work. We need and can grow from this type of relationship, even when it's imperfect—maybe *especially* when it's imperfect. Men get this; boys don't. We can learn and grow from authority figures who don't deliver feedback to us in the right way or treat us as we'd like to be treated.

I'm not suggesting we stay in abusive or unhealthy jobs. But just realize that we can learn from imperfect people—imperfect parents, imperfect coaches, imperfect bosses. Men find ways to squeeze growth out of every situation.

Authority doesn't always come in the form of a formal relationship in which one person calls all the shots. It also comes through friendships and mentorships. We need friends and mentors who will look us in the eye and say, "What you are doing is a bad idea and isn't working." This goes against the grain of our culture today. We think no one should have the right to tell us what to do. We want total freedom, even if others get hurt. Maybe this relational autonomy is part of the reason why studies show American happiness decreasing and lower than countries which place a higher value on community and interdependence.

I've found independence to be lonely, unfulfilling, and unproductive. The best teams and the best friendships happen when we develop relationships with a group of men who answer to the same code and then hold each other accountable to that code. The strongest friendships I've ever known are with men who are under the authority of Jesus and who call each other out when they stray from his code.

Jonathan and David were under the same authority. They both served the same king. More importantly, they both served the same God, and this dictated the way they lived their lives, which included honoring the authority of King Saul even when he was unworthy of it.

Many guys in our culture think they are calling their own shots when, in reality, they are submitting to the authority of the culture around them, which tells them to have no authority. I recently saw a newscast of a group of young, white males in the South pulling down a Civil War statue in a stand against racism. I'm all for standing against racism, but likely these same young men would have been pro-slavery in the South before the Civil War. They were simply imitating a popular trend.

The masses dictate our collective behavior. God goes against culture and has always been against racism. We need authorities in our lives who are under God's ways and authority and not the culture of groupthink that is anti-authority.

Our culture is giving consistent subtle and not-so-subtle cues to ignore God's authority when it comes to determining truth. Our default is to be inward focused and selfish. Again, as I mentioned earlier, just look at any men's magazine. There are no articles about how to manage your inner life or bless others or bond with others, let alone submit to others. They are about lone wolf externals, not interdependent internals.

Our best relationships, the ones that make us better and stronger at whatever we do, are those in which we give others a certain kind of authority in our lives. They're not our bosses or coaches or generals. They are something even more powerful—truth tellers. Real men give others authority in their lives by giving them permission to say the hard things. It's another form of that disconfirming evidence we looked at earlier, the "wounds from a friend" that can be trusted.

Being a man means being able to hear hard truth from friends. This is not just the your-fly-is-open kind of truth. I mean the tough stuff. You've got to be able to take a hit. There's a word the Bible uses to describe this. It's hard to hear, grates on our nerves, makes us want to walk the other way. It's a fingernails-on-a-chalkboard kind of word—*rebuke*.

Yep, I said it, rebuke—"to express sharp disapproval or criticism of (someone) because of their behavior or actions."[2] Here's one example from Paul of its use in the Bible: "I give you this charge: Preach the word; be prepared in season and out of season; correct, *rebuke* and encourage—with great patience and careful instruction" (2 Tim. 4:1–2, emphasis added).

That's not the only time the word comes up. Here are a few others:

> Let a righteous man strike me—that is a kindness;
> let him *rebuke* me—that is oil on my head. (Ps. 141:5,
> emphasis added)

> A *rebuke* impresses a discerning person
> more than a hundred lashes a fool. (Prov. 17:10, empha-
> sis added)

> Better is open *rebuke*
> than hidden love. (Prov. 27:5, emphasis added)

I could go on. In fact, the word pops up in some form about one hundred times in the Bible. Why? Because it's a critical part of a person's life. Call it rebuke, correction, criticism, admonishment, whatever. Men need hard-truth tellers in their lives, and good friends make the best ones. Even those individuals we consider great need this. Actually, *especially* the greats need this and have received it; that's why they are great. One of the clearest examples is King David, one of the greatest leaders in history. As a prepubescent teen, he chased off bears and lions while tending his family's sheep. Then he killed the giant Goliath and went on to be a warrior for the nation of Israel. He was so good at battle that his countrymen created Top 40 songs that compared him to the current king of Israel. Some of the lyrics were "Saul has killed his thousands, and David his ten thousands" (1 Sam. 18:7 NLT). His manly strength in the physical and the spiritual areas earned him relational strength with the men around him. One of them was the prophet Nathan.

But the great David also had problems, and one of them was in the sexual arena. Later in life, David and his nation were enjoying the fruits of his obedience and hard work; the country was in a time of relative peace and prosperity. David sent some of his troops out to protect the nation, but he hung back and had some idle time. One day he looked down on a neighbor's roof and noticed an attractive woman bathing. He preyed on her and had her brought to his home. He used his power to seduce her, had sex with her and conceived a child, and then tried to cover it up by having her husband, one of his loyal friends, killed.

This friend was Uriah, one of David's "mighty men." David basically killed a brother SEAL to cover up his own mistakes. In a brief period of weakness, David backslid into boyhood. He screwed up royally (literally). These were two despicable crimes in every sense of the word.

David acted like a *boy* and provided one more example of what happens when great men make boy moves. Pain is multiplied. But even in this darkness, all is not lost because David has Nathan, a man who hears from God. Because they have a relationship, Nathan calls on the king and is met warmly. He is a friend who's a truth teller in David's life. Here's what happens:

The LORD sent Nathan to David. When he came to him, he said, "There were two men in a certain town, one rich and the other poor. The rich man had a very large number of sheep and cattle, but the poor man had nothing except one little ewe lamb he had bought. He raised it, and it grew up with him and his children. It shared his food, drank from his cup and even slept in his arms. It was like a daughter to him.

"Now a traveler came to the rich man, but the rich man refrained from taking one of his own sheep or cattle to prepare a meal for the traveler who had come to him. Instead, he took the ewe lamb that belonged to the poor man and prepared it for the one who had come to him."

David burned with anger against the man and said to Nathan, "As surely as the LORD lives, the man who did this must die! He must pay for that lamb four times over, because he did such a thing and had no pity."

Then Nathan said to David, "You are the man! This is what the LORD, the God of Israel, says: 'I anointed you king over Israel, and I delivered you from the hand of Saul. I gave your master's house to you, and your master's wives into your arms. I gave you all Israel and Judah. And if all this had been too little, I would have given you even more. Why did you despise the word of the LORD by doing what is evil in his eyes? You struck down Uriah the Hittite with the sword and took his wife to be your own. You killed him with the sword of the Ammonites. Now, therefore, the sword will never depart from your house, because you despised me and took the wife of Uriah the Hittite to be your own.'

"This is what the Lord says: 'Out of your own household I am going to bring calamity on you. Before your very eyes I will take your wives and give them to one who is close to you, and he will sleep with your wives in broad daylight. You did it in secret, but I will do this thing in broad daylight before all Israel.'"

Then David said to Nathan, "I have sinned against the Lord."

Nathan replied, "The Lord has taken away your sin. You are not going to die. But because by doing this you have shown utter contempt for the Lord, the son born to you will die." (2 Sam. 12:1–14)

"You are the man!" Nathan shows radical, humble boldness and challenges his friend. Not just his friend but the king, the king who can apparently do whatever he wants and get away with it, including murder. Nathan speaks truth. He has friendship authority. That is the kind of friend we need to have in our lives. And that is the kind of friend we need to be to others. G. K. Chesterton called this the "terrible and tragic loyalty" that friends owe each other.[3]

Years ago, there were a disproportionately high number of people around me who seemed to be getting hurt by my words. I also had friends who were board members who stepped in to intercede, not only to help me with my management skills but also to protect others from being hurt by my careless words. At the time, I wasn't sure they were careless. I was convinced that the offended parties needed to lighten up and toughen up.

But some authorities in my life weren't so sure. They told me that I couldn't have a difficult conversation with anyone who reported to me without another neutral person in the room. This kept me on my best behavior and also kept the other person from potentially misrepresenting the conversation. I was also told that even if it wasn't to be a difficult conversation, I was to have a recording device with me and running for the entire interaction.

This way I would be sensitive to how I was speaking, and if there were accusations of something hurtful being said, others could listen to the recording and provide further coaching and correction.

This sounds extreme. I didn't enjoy that season of my life as a leader. But I can tell you that submitting to those authorities above me is what grew me as a man. It also helped take our team to a new level in productivity.

Respecting authorities in our lives is one of the strongest moves a guy can make. It's a key way that boys become men.

12

Boys Hold Back Emotional Expression. Men Are Affectionate.

There are a lot of unwritten rules to manhood. The problem is a lot of them were written by boys and are just plain stupid: men don't show weakness; men don't cry; and here in the United States, maybe the biggest of them all, men don't show affection to one another.

Growing up, the only times my friends touched me were if they were tackling me, punching me in the shoulder, or kicking me in the nuts.

As we age, we start shaking hands. As the friendship advances, we do the handshake that seamlessly morphs into a choreographed hug as we pull the guy forward and give two back slaps before we release. On very rare circumstances we go directly to the two-armed hug. But I will never greet another man with a kiss. I wish I could, especially when I read verses such as "Greet one another with a holy kiss" (2 Cor. 13:12).

There was a time in American culture, however, when men showed affection to their friends. If you look at old photos of nineteenth-century American men, you see great expressions of friendship through touch: arms around each other, holding hands in group photos, even sitting on each other's laps. Some want to explain these as homosexual behavior, but the evidence is clear that they were widespread, culturally accepted expressions among heterosexual men as signs of friendship. They also ended letters to each other with phrases such as "very affectionately yours."

I'm not sure why expressing affection has changed so significantly since then. Some would say it was the outcome of a war creating a generation of emotionally wounded and repressed fathers and grandfathers. Sure, why not? Let's go ahead and add it to the list of stuff we can blame our parents for: bankrupt social security, runaway healthcare costs, disco music, and repressed male emotions.

We don't see these touch-starved male friendships in other parts of the world. One of the unexpected twists my life has taken is that I now work in places around the world that previously had not even crossed my mind—from small townships in South Africa to megacities in India to rural villages in Nicaragua. Much of it is culture shock in a very healthy way as I see God working in ways that are very different from the little American box I put him in.

One of the things I've noticed is how male friendships play out in some very different ways from my experience. Male friends hold hands as they walk down the street in India. Men greet each other with a kiss in an Arab country. These kinds of expressions can come as a shock to Americans, who default to all physical touch as being sexual. I remember when President Bush hosted Prince (soon to be King) Abdullah of Saudi Arabia at his ranch in Crawford, Texas, in 2005. Some were shocked when he greeted the prince with a kiss and then proceeded to lead him around holding his hand, both signs of respect and affection.

But still our twenty-first-century American culture treats non-sexual expressions of affection, particularly between male friends, as somehow weak or weird or evidence of being gay.

On some level, American guys realize we're missing out. It's not that we're not trying to be more physically expressive. We've developed the high five, the fist bump, the chest bump, and even jumping up and banging our sides into each other. This is the best we've come up with so far, but we're working on it.

In the Bible, we see a story about David, one of the manliest men in recorded history, openly weeping and showing affection to his friend, Jonathan: "David rose from beside the stone heap and fell on his face to the ground and bowed three times. And they kissed one another and wept with one another, David weeping the most" (1 Sam. 20:41 ESV). In our culture, this is thought to be unmanly.

Elsewhere in the Bible we see Esau greeting his brother Jacob with a hug and a kiss (Gen. 33:4), Peter telling his friends to "greet one another with a kiss of love" (1 Pet. 5:14), and Paul's friends and fellow church workers saying good-bye to him with hugs, kisses, and tears (Acts 20:37).

And then there's the classic parable Jesus told of a father's radical love for his wayward son. The man's son had not only demanded his inheritance early but had also gone off and squandered it partying. And then he came crawling home. But in the story, Jesus says that when the father saw his son "a long way off," he "was filled with compassion for him; he ran to his son, threw his arms around him and kissed him" (Luke 15:20). Over and over in the Bible we see that close relationships between men, between brothers, between fathers and sons, and between friends are physically affectionate.

We are missing something. There is a power to nonsexual affection, including physical touch, that we are missing. Child development researchers have found that the need for physical contact with another human being is critical to infant development. Sometimes this learning has come through tragic circumstances, such as among orphans in a wide range of deplorable conditions in Eastern Europe. The commonality of their experience of lack of human physical touch contributed to impaired growth, cognitive development, and even elevated levels of infection.

Physical and affectionate touch has been shown to improve our heart rate, blood pressure, and cortisol levels. The hippocampus, which houses our memories, is stimulated and releases a host of chemicals that lead to positive and uplifting emotions. Our inner skull can't be touched by hands, but our brain chemistry bubbles with affectionate touch. Nor is physical affection only emotional in nature; it is also a spiritual thing that affects us physically.

As I mentioned earlier, the suicide rate is three to four times higher among young males than young females. One of the theories for why this is so is that girls receive more touch from their parents and one another and thus have more emotional needs met. Girls willingly hug each other, hold hands, and even dance with one another at high school events. A young male has cultural restrictions on all the above actions and therefore misses out on some of the benefits of affection, which could go a long way toward warding off problems that often lead to suicide.

We all know that children need affectionate touch. But we need more than only caring childhood environments; we need *every* environment to have plenty of human touch. In fact, the older I get the more I feel the need of it. Yet our culture continues to tell young males that touching is inappropriate, and as they grow older they get lonelier and lonelier, until they get to the place where an adult male can go days or weeks without touching another human being.

It's become a bit of a cliché to cite the number of very driven, successful guys who are empty on the inside because all their drive comes from trying to replace the father's embrace they never received. Unfortunately, it's also true and is the experience of many men.

I have a friend who made it a point to hug his young daughter at least once every day, and stuck with it even through the squirming teenage years. He said he wanted her to know he loved her and hoped that every caring, loving touch she got from him might be one less that she went looking for in an unhealthy place.

We all need touch—healthy, friendship touch.

13

Boys Make Each Other Comfortable.
Men Make Each Other Better.

A friend of mine, Matt, and his wife invited us to go to their place on the Ohio River for New Year's. We were going to sleep over, and in the morning I was to go duck hunting on the river with Matt. I'm not a big hunter; it's not my thing. But he'd already obtained the license for me, said some other guys were coming along, and convinced me it would be fun. So I agreed. Matt and his friends, however, are really into it.

When we got up on New Year's Day, it was only ten degrees. Matt said we had to get out on the lake early because, as he put it, "Ducks are stupid at sunrise." I looked like the Stay Puft Marshmallow Man; I had every layer of clothes in my possession on my body. It was ridiculously cold.

Once we got on the water, Matt pulled out the decoys and started tossing them out. Each one had a little anchor on it. Then, he pulled the boat over to the shore. From the side of the boat, we ducked behind blinds, which were supposed to keep the ducks from seeing us. Then we sat there with our guns and tobacco, waiting for something to happen.

Since I was a newbie, I was in observation mode. I noticed that whenever a flock flew overhead, Matt pulled out his duck call. I asked, "Why and how does this work—the decoys, the calls, and stuff?"

He said, "Well, ducks are social creatures. They like to make friends."

So these ducks are flying high, thinking, *I got to get down south. I got to get down south.* Then they hear the duck call and look down. *Hey! Is that Bill and Stella down there? Maybe, maybe not, but I'm totally up for making new friends right now. Let's go!*

Just before they hit the water, they spread their wings to slow down—and make a nice big target. Three guys pop up out of the boat and shoot. BOOM! BOOM! BOOM! Awesome. God bless America! The bummer is we didn't hit a single duck all morning. I have no clue how that happened.

But here's the reason I told this story: men in real friendships give their friends a license to kill things that need to be killed in their lives. When you share experiences with other men, and are accountable to and vulnerable with them, you can say, "If you see something in my life that you think needs to die, you have a license to tell me anytime, anywhere." The Bible says, "As iron sharpens iron, so one person sharpens another (Prov. 27:17). Men make one another tougher, sharper, more focused. I can't imagine where I'd be if friends hadn't called out behavior in my life that needed to change. Men give their friends a hunting license.

This is one aspect of the friendship authority we talked about in chapter 11. Men realize teams are much stronger than individuals. This is especially true when it comes to blinds we hide behind and our blind spots. Several years ago, Michael Lewis's book (and later movie) *The Blind Side* centered on Michael Oher and highlighted why the position of left tackle is so critical in the NFL. Since most quarterbacks are right-handed, when they drop back to pass, their back is turned to the left side. This is their blind side, the area they can't see and their biggest vulnerability. The left tackle's job is to protect their blind side. Protecting the team's most valuable and expensive player against the opposing team's largest and quickest players is a high-paying job that few can handle. They have their quarterback's back.

We all have our blind sides. Maybe for you it's a tendency to drift into unhealthy work habits at the expense of your family. There are seasons in our work when we have to make sacrifices, but a real friend can call our attention to the fact that the season has now gone on for two years. Maybe it's a temptation to have one too many beers. Maybe it's the way you talk to your wife. We all have our blind sides and need to give our friends permission to call them out. It's a rare guy, regardless of how close they are to you, that will step into that space without permission. But if you give your closest friends that kind of hunting license, you will be amazed at what you learn.

I have an entrepreneur friend who was considering a big career shift a few years ago. He was working for a company that was doing well financially, but he was increasingly uncomfortable with some of the choices the ownership was making. He considered leaving and launching out on his own. It wasn't a no-brainer though. It would be a risky financial move, and he had a wife and kids to provide for. He also knew he had control issues that had kept him from taking appropriate risks.

For the average guy, the story ends with coming to a decision by talking it over with his wife and the two of them sweating the decision on their own. (The wife part is critical. You can't skip that step.) But my friend also called together me and a couple other close friends. He laid out the situation, told us how he was processing it, then asked us for a couple of things. First, he asked to hear any input we might have, especially about pieces he might be missing or seeing in a skewed way (the confirmation bias we talked about in chap. 8). Second, he asked us to pray for him as he and his wife worked through the decision. Then he gave us permission to ask him anything or challenge him on anything over the next couple of months in regard to this decision. He gave us hunting licenses.

I greatly respect the craft of singles tennis players. I also admire the discipline and toughness of wrestlers who go one-on-one with another person in front of a crowd. But those athletic pursuits never catch my imagination like team sports, especially football. A friend of mine once described an experience he had while coaching an NFL team, which shall remain nameless. He described a game early in the season when they got blown out. They did their best to learn from the loss but couldn't put too much time into the film because they had to prepare for the next week. Later in the season they had a second game against that team.

When they were reviewing film in the week leading up to the second game, they realized the key to their loss had been a single player who regularly blew his assignment on plays and went with his gut instead. The player was a stud talent; he just wanted to do his own thing. They eventually replaced him because not following the plays became a trend, and they couldn't continue to compensate around him. Every part of the game plan, on both sides of the ball, had been affected. With the exception of that one player, they went into the second game with the same team *and* the exact same game plan. And they won handily. One player doing his own thing had brought down the others. That's what happens in a team sport. No one wins Super Bowls with eleven or twenty-two or fifty-three independent players.

Boys make each other comfortable. Men make each other better.

14

Boys Tear Each Other Down.
Men Build Each Other Up.

Encouragement makes us smarter.

Well, kind of. In his book, *The Social Neuroscience of Education*, Pepperdine's Louis Cozolino said that receiving encouragement has been shown to actually stimulate the brain's ability to change.[1] The ability to change our brains has become a popular area of research lately. It's what they call neuroplasticity, and it can result in improved performance across a wide range of areas. I'll leave the brain science to the PhDs, but in my own life, I've definitely experienced mental change following a word of encouragement.

The first day of practice on my junior high football team, I bumped into a coach from my peewee team. He said, "We are watching you, and you are going to do great." I floated away from that interaction and drew from those words numerous times when I was on the field. I'm sure those words knocked a half second off my time in the forty-yard dash.

The first week on the job at the church I serve, Jim Bechtold who hired me said, "Brian, some people have talent for playground sports and some can play at the varsity level. Others can compete in college. But you have Olympic level, world-class talent. God is going to do huge things with you." I'm still not sure that he was accurate, but I am sure that his encouragement elevated my game and caused me to be a better version of myself.

Shortly after my oldest daughter graduated from college, she felt compelled to share with me some things that went on in college that she hadn't been transparent about. She confessed experiences she had, lies she told, and decisions she made that were painful and which she regretted. It was a very tender and vulnerable move on her part. It was stuff that I would almost prefer not to know. Definitely stuff I wish had never happened. At the end of her confession, I tried my best to impart grace, understanding, remorse, and fatherly wisdom. In tears she said, "You are a great dad. You are truly the best dad I could ever have." That served as encouragement that stiffened my resolve to be a godly man for my kids as they age.

At some level, I think we all know the positive juice that encouragement can be for a boy. Done correctly, it gives boys confidence to try new things, the grit to stick with the hard stuff, and the resilience to get back up when they're knocked down. Encouragement is protein for a boy's growth. This is known as "predictive affirmation," in which people rise to a respected figure's expectation of them or, conversely, turn negative expectations into self-fulfilling prophecies.

I'm not talking about positive thinking mumbo jumbo or blaming missing our January sales quota on the fact our parents didn't get us that Evel Knievel stunt cycle when we were nine. What I do know is that encouragement *can* actually help us grow into something we currently aren't. And it doesn't stop with boys. As hard as it is for some guys to admit, we still need that kind of nutrition as men.

Encouragement is when you put strength and courage into somebody. That's literally what the word means. Boys can't encourage, because they harbor a sick sense of competition that fears making someone else stronger, as if life was graded on a curve. If they can't raise their own game but can at least knock or hold others down, they'll be better off. This, by the way, isn't just a challenge for guys.

My friend Nancy says one of the biggest problems in female friendships is the tendency to compare their lives rather than share their lives. For boys, this usually takes the form of mocking and teasing one another. There's nothing wrong with having fun with one another. (I consider it a spiritual gift of mine!) But the basis of a relationship should be affirmation, knowing you are on the same team and are fans of each other. The core of your interaction should say, "I'm thankful that you're in my life, and I want to show you by building you up."

We see this again and again in the Bible. The apostle Paul was big on encouragement. His letters were full of affirmation. He told one of the churches he helped start in the city of Thessalonica to "encourage one another and build one another up" (1 Thess. 5:11 ESV). He knew that his fellow followers of Jesus were living in a time when people around them thought they were weird (sound familiar?). He also knew that one of the best ways to counteract feelings of isolation was for them to continuously strengthen each other with encouragement.

I like to give nicknames. I'm not sure exactly why. I like to think it is a manly thing to do.

Darin is a daring executive pastor. He is Daredevil.

Steven wanders in and out of meetings. He is Kitty.

Kathy is a strong older woman. She is the Iron Lady.

Jerry is the oldest person on our board. He is Jerry-atric.

Mike is always happy. He is Sunshine.

Steve wore a motorcycle jacket that smelled as disgusting as wearing sausage links stuffed with poop around his neck. He is Link.

Craig always has greasy hair; he must just squirt Windex on it, and so he is.

Jay reminds me of Kimbo Slice. He is Kimbo.

Tye can do a lot of things. He is Multi.

Andy is resourceful. He is Handy.

Joe Lee is Angelina.

Josh changes his look often. He is the Riddler.

My neighbor Dan is a big guy. He is Danimal.

Chad has no expression on his face. He is Bo (for Botox).

Andrew is an entrepreneur who spends too much money on clothes. He would make *EQ* magazine, and so he is.

Some nicknames are created simply because I like to say them.

Molly is McNutter Butter.
Liz is Lizard.
Matt Welty is Scabby.
Mark is Mark My Word.
Another Mark is Marky Mark.
Talaria is Malaria.
Sylvia is Saliva.

What can I say? It's a gift. Maybe it goes back to growing up in Pittsburgh in the 1970s. When you're a kid and your team wins four Super Bowls in six years, it does something to you. And it wasn't just the wins; it was also the nicknames. Those were platinum years for killer nicknames: The Steel Curtain, Iron Mike Webster,

Mean Joe Greene, Dwight "Mad Dog" White. Those were the days. Today we get attempts like "Ocho-Cinco," which doesn't count on the basis that a guy can't give himself a nickname, and Matty Ice, which sounds more like a Teletubby. No, sir. Pittsburgh in the 1970s was a time when men had real nicknames that meant something (although I do have to give Beast Mode and Megatron honorable mention).

I do have some company in nicknaming—God. There are multiple times in the Bible when God says in so many words, "Yeah, I know your mom calls you this, but I'm going to call you this." In Genesis he told Abram that his name was now Abraham because he was going to be the father of nations (17:5). Later, we see Jesus doing this when he told his friend and disciple Simon his name was now Peter (which means rock), and on this rock he would build his church (Matt. 16:18). I wonder how Peter handled this. I mean, come on, Jesus starts calling you the Rock. What guy would mind that? I wonder if the other disciples were jealous. Maybe they kept calling him Simon, and Peter had to remind them, "Hey guys, you heard the man. I'm the Rock now; call me the Rock."

My all-time favorite nickname, though, is the one Jesus gave to John and James. Jesus had gathered his core team (who would themselves end up with a top-ten nickname: the twelve disciples) and was giving them the authority to do all kinds of things in his name. Then he gave James and his brother John the nickname Boanerges, which means "Sons of Thunder" (Mark 3:17). Now there's a nickname. Any name that would work equally well on the back of a leather jacket and as a fantasy football team is a keeper. Hands-down, best nickname ever. I bet they couldn't wait to see Peter's reaction. "Hey, Rock, did you hear that? Sons of Thunder!" Mic drop.

If you go back and read each of these stories closely, you'll see that each of the nicknames—Abraham, the Rock, Sons of Thunder—have something in common. They were all names of encouragement. They were all names that called out something great, something truly awesome in each of these guys.

And maybe the best part is that they were all names that encouraged them to be something they weren't yet perfect at. They were just becoming it. Abraham, the "father of nations," was ninety-nine years old with no kids when God renamed him. Peter had not shown many rock-like tendencies and would, in fact, fold under pressure and deny he even knew Jesus not long after. James and John's work was just beginning as they would go on to be solid leaders in the early church. The new name was affirmation, a shot of encouragement, a statement from someone who knew them and loved them and knew who they were created to be—predictive affirmation.

I have a friend who used to coach kindergarten soccer. He had a boy on his team that was a little bit chunkier and slower than the others. We'll call him Bill. What Bill lacked in natural ability, he more than made up for in hustle and fearlessness. My neighbor put Bill in the role of center fullback. He was the last line of defense before the goalkeeper. Bill was neither fast nor nimble, but he turned out to be a stud defender. He wouldn't let anyone get past him.

After the first game, a shutout, my friend called out Bill's play and said, "Bill, no one could get around you out there. You were like a rock. That's what you were out there, a rock! You're the rock." Bill's eyes lit up. His mom later said he was never the same. A week later, one of the other moms came to my friend and said that all of the boys were calling Bill "the rock" and that they wanted nicknames too. And so my friend came up with a nickname for each of the boys that called out what was best in them.

There's something about encouragement. And for guys, encouragement is most powerful when it comes from an authority figure or a friend who knows us well.

We talked earlier about the value of having friends who are truth tellers in our lives and the value of our being a truth teller in their lives. We've probably all been in some kind of work training in which we've been told the best way to deliver criticism to someone is to first give them a compliment, then the criticism, and end with another compliment. They call it the "C" sandwich. I'm not a big fan of that method because I think most people can smell the criticism coming from a mile away, and as a result the compliments come off as fake and manipulative. The principle is right though. We grow best when tough challenges come from voices who have a track record of encouraging us. Strong friendships, strong men are built on affirmation.

I'm big on guys finding a spiritual community, a church they can be part of, contribute to, and be challenged by. I know my community, Crossroads, is exactly that for me and my friends. And because we gather together in large groups, our scale and diversity help us make a dent in things in a way that my family and close friends alone can't. I believe that churches—small, medium, and large—are channels of God's love to our cities and world. But I also know there's a certain kind of encouragement we don't get in large groups. It's the affirmation that comes one-on-one from a friend who knows us well, someone who knows us, warts and all, and still loves us.

Listen, men, don't think that you can go it alone. If you want to move from boyhood to manhood, you have to choose to be part of a team. You need strong, affectionate, active, authoritative, accountable, affirming friends in your life, and you need to be those things for other men.

117

15

Boys Live to Play.
Men Play to Live.

In one of my favorite moments, I'm about eight feet in the air, my back to the ground, and dropping like a rock. I'm also gripping my six-year-old son in a tight bear hug with both my arms. We've morphed into a single father-son ball and are bracing for impact. And there's nothing but joy on our faces. It's a trampoline game we used to play after dinner when my kids were young. I would wrap them up in a tight grip and launch us off the trampoline. Once in the air, I would fall backward and we would plummet back down, me staring at the sky and my kid staring over my shoulder at the quickly approaching landing. As we hit and bounced, their face would come within an inch of the tramp surface. Talk about a good time. I can't believe they don't have a picture of that move on the cover of trampoline brochures. Those are such sweet memories. Actually, to be honest, they are bittersweet.

Every time I think of those days, I'm reminded of how much fun we had as a family on that trampoline after dinner. I also remember how my kids had to almost drag me out there and how that was about the only time I made room for that kind of play. I was in my thirties, running hard, building a new church, trying to make my mark on the world, and not making much time for silly things like play. I was wrong about play.

And the Church (I mean, big "C" church consisting of all believers everywhere) wasn't much help. In a lot of the religious circles I had been exposed to growing up, the informal understanding was that the closer you got to God, the more serious and dull you became. In fact, if someone around you was having a good time, they must be doing something wrong. And the ones who did squeeze a little fun in here and there (poker night, bowling, dancing . . . careful there, Tiger) almost felt like they had to apologize for it. It's as if they were playing recklessly in a giant, unfinished basement just waiting for Dad to storm down the stairs and tell them to "cut it out!" The Church was wrong about play.

And play is something that for the most part this great country we live in doesn't get much better. What often passes for play is just another goal-obsessed, over-scheduled activity that stands out from the other six days of goal-obsessed, over-scheduled madness only because we're wearing running shoes or a jersey.

I think that may be why the 2017 World Happiness Report showed that the United States doesn't even crack the top ten in happiest countries. We're number fourteen. That's right, fourteen. Three spots below Israel and seven spots below Canada.[1] Israel—a little strip of land surrounded by people who want to destroy them; a place where parents have to teach their children how to wear a gas mask. These people are happier than we are. And Canada—I'll give them hockey and maple syrup, but we've got every other sport, Bruce Springsteen, and deep-dish pizza. We should be winning the happiness game. We're not. We're barely in the sweet sixteen of Happiness March Madness. Our country is wrong about play.

The problem is we think that play is something that helps boys become men but then should stop there. Whether it's dodgeball on the playground, the board game Risk at our best friend's dining room table, or late-summer football camp two-a-days in full pads, we believe play stops when we grow up. This faulty logic says a mark of a man is that he stops all play. This is wrong. Play not only helps boys grow into men but also helps men grow *as* men.

What follows is my MANifesto on play: five reasons why men should play.

Play Replenishes Our Power

It's a little surprising that our country has lost its appreciation of play given our focus on renewable energy. What is renewable energy? It's energy that is naturally replenished, such as hydroelectric, solar, geothermal, and so on.

That's exactly what play is to us. It's renewable energy for a man's heart, mind, and soul. Here's how a group led by Dr. Stuart Brown describes it:

> Play is the gateway to vitality. By its nature it is uniquely and intrinsically rewarding. It generates optimism, seeks out novelty, makes perseverance fun, leads to mastery, gives the immune system a bounce, fosters empathy, and promotes a sense of belonging and community. Each of these play by-products are indices of personal health, and their shortage predicts impending health problems and personal fragility.[2]

And yes, there really is such a thing as the National Institute for Play, and Dr. Brown is a *medical* doctor. He's trained in general and internal medicine, psychiatry, and clinical research. He first recognized the importance of play by discovering its absence in the life history of murderers and felony drunk drivers.

Play is the antidote to tension. It's revenge on a stress-filled world that tries to beat us down. Play makes us healthier men. It's renewable energy. It replenishes our power.

Play Puts Me in My Place

We're probably all familiar with the biblical creation story in the book of Genesis. You may believe that the seven days and evenings and mornings were the same then as our current definition of those terms, or you may interpret the time frame differently. Here, I just want to point out the sequence.

> So God created man in his own image,
>   in the image of God he created them;
>   male and female he created them. . . .

God saw all that he had made, and it was very good. And there was evening, and there was morning—the sixth day. (Gen. 1:27, 31)

God created man on the sixth day. And then what happened? What came next? "And God blessed the seventh day and made it holy, because on it he rested from all the work of creating that he had done" (Gen. 2:3).

God created humans on day six, and what's the first order of business for these go-getters, the original pioneers, creators, and builders? It's *not* work. Call it rest, relaxation, play, or whatever you'd like. It's a day of *not work*. Seems a little weird, doesn't it? The clear picture we get of God is that he's all-powerful. He's infinite power and energy. It's not likely he needed to take a breather. And it was Adam and Eve's first full day of existence. They hadn't yet worked a day in their lives. They certainly didn't need a day off.

God's institution of nonproductive activity reminds us that he wants us to be human beings, not human doings. His institution of rest on that first day means that we rest to work rather than rest from our work. The power to get things done comes when we are rested; we don't rest only when we are worn out.

Jesus gives us another angle on rest when he says, "The Sabbath was made for man, not man for the Sabbath" (Mark 2:27). God was starting them off with nonproductivity to remind them they were not the masters of the universe. Yes, God wanted them to be productive, but they were put here to connect with God, and out of *that* comes the strength and power and creativity to be productive.

And so it is for us. The concept of Sabbath refers to a regular, one-day-a-week-minimum scheduled time of nonproductivity, of rest and play, of activity that brings us joy and is removed from whatever pays the bills or reminds us of our role at work. It is necessary for our spiritual sanity and physical health. Recreation is a bit of *re*-creation—restoring, renewing, and reminding us we are not the source of our energy. When I take time to play, I send a very healthy message to God: *I know who's in control of the universe, and it's not me. I'm not that important.*

Play puts us in our place.

Play Stokes Passion

Science tells us that those of us who don't play are more fixed and rigid in our responses to complex stimuli. As a result, we don't seek out novelty and newness and have less ability to adapt. It appears that our emotional and physical nimbleness is directly tied to our aptitude to play. Dr. Brown says, "When adults don't play much, the consequences are rigidity, depression, lack of adaptability, loss of irony, and such."[3]

The irony is that not playing enough can actually lower our effectiveness at work. Early in Google's life, they encouraged their engineers to take 20 percent of their time to work on something outside of their regular job projects. It could be anything they found interesting that might also have some application for the company. Google has since evolved their policy, but that 20 percent of time resulted in such creations as Gmail, Google Earth, and Google News.

The predecessor of this idea was 3M's "15 percent time" that allowed employees to use a portion of their paid time to chase rainbows and hatch their own ideas. One innovation that came out of it began when one of their scientists, Art Frey, became frustrated by trying to keep the bookmarks in place in his church hymnal at choir practice. He worked on applying an adhesive dreamed up by one of his colleagues, Spencer Silver, to a new kind of note paper that they eventually called the Post-It Note, launching a billion-dollar annual business, not to mention a slew of office pranks and cheap Halloween costumes.

Nonproductive time just might make us more productive than ever. Google mandated 20 percent, 3M mandated 15 percent, and God mandates a minimum of 14 percent (one day in seven) in order to restore us and stoke our passion.

Play Purges Unhealthy Desires

I'm getting to the age at which I've collected more than a few stories of peers who have spiraled downward, guys who by almost all measures were succeeding. They were strong, effective, and had great families.

And then they crashed—emotionally or morally or both. Unfortunately, my mental database of these stories seems to grow every year. And I've noticed a trend. Almost every one of them was lacking any regular time for play or pleasure in their life. Men, we may think we're the exception to this, but the data is very clear: if we don't regularly play and experience pleasure, it's only a matter of time before something unhealthy causes us to fall. In fact, it's a pretty good rule of thumb that whenever we start thinking we're the exception to the rule, watch out.

We are wired for pleasure. Our taste buds aren't there just to figure out if a berry is poisonous. God gave us taste buds so we could have pleasure eating food. We are created for pleasure, and one way or another we will find pleasure. It will either be in healthy, planned ways or it will be in unhealthy, spontaneous ways—for example, the workaholic guy who has an adulterous affair with his coworker or the pastor who has nowhere to let his hair down except in private on his back deck with his buddy Jack Daniels.

Healthy play not only *re*-creates us physically, mentally, and emotionally but also serves as a vaccine. It makes unhealthy play less appealing. It helps purge unhealthy desires. If you don't play, you are more at risk for addictions, affairs, and a whole lot of other self-inflicted diseases.

Show me a guy who doesn't play in public and I'll show you a guy who's going to play in private. Play purges unhealthy desires.

Play Pleases God

I don't remember ever having a baseball or football game that my dad did not attend. It didn't matter if it was bad weather or I was not slated to start. He was always there. I remember looking up at him in the rain and thinking, "Why does he do this? I wouldn't." And then I had my own kids.

It is amazing the amount of joy I had helping Lena learn how to pitch a softball for her first grade team and later learn how to play tennis.

When Jake played football, my eyes were locked on him in every play. I could tell his walk from a mile away even if he was wearing a helmet and a different jersey number.

In Moriah's last high school softball season, making games that were likely to be blowouts one way or the other was a priority. Why? Because it brought me great satisfaction seeing my child on the field of play having a good time.

It's the same with our Father God. We have been created in his image, and we share his DNA. Watching his son on a four-wheeler or in a deer stand or finger painting or rehabbing a muscle car makes him smile. He very well may say to the angels around him, "That's my boy!"

In a letter to a young guy named Timothy whom he was mentoring, the apostle Paul gave this counsel: "As for the rich in this present age, charge them not to be haughty, nor to set their hopes on the uncertainty of riches, but on God, who richly provides us with everything to enjoy" (1 Tim. 6:17 ESV). Many who read this verse may see only the charge for the wealthy not to be arrogant or put their hope in their money, and that's definitely true. But let's not miss that God "richly provides us with everything to enjoy." He enjoys our enjoyment. He takes pleasure in our pleasure. From the "trees that were pleasing to the eye" (Gen. 2:9) to our times of rest and play, we please God when we enjoy what he has given us.

I believe that one of the reasons I've been fruitful in the same job for twenty-one-plus years is because of spending time on motorcycles. I believe that one of the reasons my three kids, who have all moved out of the house, want to spend time with me is because when we are together we have fun. Play is a magnet that draws kids to their dads.

I also believe that one of the reasons men aren't drawn to church or to Jesus is because they don't see other men who are actually having fun. *Only* keeping rules and being "good" isn't attractive to our friends, nor does it align with God's plan for our lives.

Men don't grow out of the need to play. In fact, a man who is all work and no play is a boy headed for trouble. We need to take control of our lives and realize we aren't immune to heartache;

nor are we immortal. We need to spend an adequate amount of our time and money on play.

Your Dad in heaven doesn't want to see you redlining. He isn't impressed with another accomplishment or accommodation. You've proven to him that you aren't a slacker. Now give him joy by seeing his son play and allow yourself to fully experience the life he has blessed you with.

— — —

NOW DO SOMETHING

Read about the value of friendships in Proverbs 27:17.

Questions to Consider

1. Are you living as a lone wolf, or are you part of a pack? What activity could you do with other men in order to connect? How could you make that a regular thing?

2. When is the last time you let down your guard and let another man know what you were truly feeling—whether it be anger, fear, sadness, excitement, or joy?

3. Who or what is the ultimate authority in your life, and do you regularly connect with other men who answer to the same authority?

4. To whom do you need to grant a hunting license to freely call out things they see in your life that might need addressing? When will you do it?

5. For whom can you be an important source of encouragement this week?

MARK IV

MEN WORK

16

Boys Don't Want to Work. Men Work.

Often, companies that are selling something will tell us whatever we want to hear in order to get us to buy. I was recently at Chipotle, and I saw this quote on the side of a bag: "Hope that in the future, all is well, everyone eats free, no one must work, all just sit around feeling love to each other."

Doesn't that sound like a great future? No, it sounds like a *miserable* future. Today, many of us have a distorted view of work. There is a growing sentiment in our culture that work is somehow evil. If we didn't have to work, things would be better, and we would have more time for love. This sentiment is not good. If you don't work, you don't eat, and you aren't being loving to those who need you.

This view is also contrary to what we see in the Bible and in the lives of every respectable man I know. In fact, we first see the value of work in the first chapter of the Bible. God is creating, working, forming, separating light from dark and water from land, and making things that didn't previously exist. At the end of each day, the Bible says, "God saw all that he had made, and it was very good" (Gen. 1:31).

What was good? His work. God worked, and it was *good*. Why is it good? Because work is inherently good. Work makes things happen. Work improves reality. Work begets innovation that solves problems. Work shapes our character. Work makes us like God.

In my first job, as a paperboy, I learned to do the same repetitive tasks over and over with consistency. "Oh, it's raining out? Too bad! Deliver the papers." This was a critical character trait that still serves me to this day.

My next job was working at Hardee's, back when fast-food workers wore orange and brown polyester. And in that nonbreathable fabric, I slapped frozen patties onto a flaming grill as my clothes seemed to melt to my body. At closing, I carried seventy-pound buckets of previously boiling grease out to an Exxon Valdez–looking container. One night I forgot to wear my rubber apron, and I spilled the grease *way* too close to my private parts and ended up with second-degree burns over the bottom half of my body. (Thank you, Jesus, for the near miss!) It was never an easy day, and I learned the value of enduring through difficulty.

In another job, I was a caterer. This job gave me my first entry point into the world of diversity. Up till then, I'd been around only people who were mostly like me; the man who owned the catering company was gay. It was my first experience with people whose life experiences weren't like mine.

When I started working in construction, I had some tough jobs such as backfilling, tearing off roofs, and siding buildings. What I loved about the job was that at the end of the day I could point to something tangible and say, "I did that." (Today, there are fewer opportunities to point at things and say the same because most of my work is with people, and the payoff is much longer term.) But through my construction job, I learned the value of hard work in the midst of dirty and inglorious projects.

Boys, however, don't want to work. They want to play all the time. They want to do what feels fun in the moment, and because of this they not only fail to grow as men but also miss out on the blessings that God has for us through work.

Boys love books with titles such as *The 4-Hour Workweek*. When they do work, it is so they can retire early so they don't have to do any more work. Sure, our workloads may change throughout our lives, and the kind of work we do will change, but let's be clear: *not* working is never a goal of a respectable and mature man.

In all my jobs, God taught me skills that I still use today. Every day I do repetitive stuff I don't want to do, I endure through difficulties, and I interact with and lead people who don't see the world as I do. Those early work experiences shaped how I engage to this very day.

Work isn't just about building wealth. It is also about building people, especially our families.

Easter bums me out. Not the Jesus-coming-back-from-the-dead part but the Easter basket part. My wife loves showering my kids with love and presents. There is Santa Claus and also Easter Claus when my wife is on the scene. I think she spends too much money on stuff to fill their baskets. It is one thing when it is chocolate at age eight, but when it is gift cards and other expensive gifts jammed in a basket at age eighteen, my eyes roll.

Once the youngest turned turned eighteen and the others were twenty-three and twenty-five, I assumed my traditional role of creating clues to lead them to their baskets was over. When they were younger it was great fun seeing them go from place to place in the house following clues that contained the Easter story and directional advice. Here is one example:

Jesus had a meal and then was painfully arrested.
What else could he possibly do?

133

But Judas's garden kiss caused him to be tested.

Your first clue is where Dad takes a poo.

(That's good stuff right there and there are more where that came from.) My kids weren't happy to hear me say on that fateful Easter afternoon, "I don't have any clues for you. I thought you had grown out of that game." I'll never forget my oldest daughter droning, "Well, that sucks!"

I was convicted about no longer carrying on the family tradition. This wasn't a manly move. The next year we started the Easter basket hunt tradition back up, except now the clues run them all over the city of Cincinnati.

You never stop working at being a Dad. Why? Because men work.

17

Boys Work to Stake Claims.
Men Work to Experience God.

One of our biggest problems with work is expectation management. I don't mean we expect too much from it. I think we expect too little. We're looking to work to bring us cars and food and houses and maybe even fame and fortune. And sometimes it does. These are not bad things. But when that's all we're looking for, we're aiming way too low.

Boys love the bumper sticker I Owe, I Owe, So Off to Work I Go. Is that what it has come to? We only work because we have made bad financial decisions? That is an attitude that will sink our drive to be a man who produces something of value, which comes about through work. Jesus says, "My Father is always working, and so am I" (John 5:17 NLT).

Last night I celebrated my birthday with my adult children. We were reliving old memories and my nineteen-year-old said, "All my memories of you on your day off when I was little are of you wearing a tool belt." The others chimed in and recounted various projects we worked on together as we were building a house to inhabit or rehabbing our house to sell. They were always around, holding a board or carrying a bucket. Oftentimes, their presence hurt my productivity. They would see various tools and use them to bang on things that should have been painted instead. But in those times, I never got too mad because I wanted my kids around, and they wanted to be around me. That is part of what happens when we work. Productivity will hopefully increase, but relationships absolutely increase when we work with others.

The primary reason we work is to experience God.

In the book of Genesis, when God created Adam and Eve he gave them some responsibilities. The Bible says, "And God blessed them. And God said to them, 'Be fruitful and multiply and fill the earth and subdue it'" (Gen. 1:28 ESV).

The first part? Be fruitful and multiply? That's some good work right there! Yep, I'll sign up for that one. But what does it mean to subdue the earth?

In the very next chapter of Genesis, sin is going to enter the world. Adam and Eve disobey God, and that's when everything goes south. Cancer, death, pollution, confusing NFL rule changes, and everything else bad enters the world. But notice this: God's plan for them to work came *before* all of that. The earth wasn't out of control yet, but God commanded them to work. Work is not bad. It's a part of the natural order. *It's what God planned for us.*

God commanded Adam and Eve to create order out of creation. He commanded them to bring culture and civilization into being. They were to figure out how to manage it, organize it, and make things that didn't yet exist. They had to figure out how to take a stick and a tendon from an animal and create an instrument to make music, for example. All this happens through work.

God works, so when we put our hand to the plow, in a very real way we are experiencing a part of him we can't in other ways. Years ago I read the classic book *Experiencing God* by Henry Blackaby and Claude King, and it impacted the way I think about my work. They said that if you're wondering what to do with your life, a great first step is to look where God's work is happening and to go be a part of it.[1] Not bad advice. If you want to experience God, go where he is and help out. Is there a company with great potential and a mission that God would embrace? Apply for a job. Is somebody feeding the poor nearby? Go help them. Are there struggling kids in underresourced schools? Mentor one of them. Is there a widow on your street? Cut her grass. And if there's a way you can take your unique skill set and serve others *and* make money doing it, go for it.

If we set the bar at using work only to provide money, we are likely to get knocked off course in the journey of manliness. Even a third grade boy will embrace work long enough to earn a lollipop. Lollipops become expensive toys and vacations for many fifty-five-year-old boys who have rewards absent a healthy spiritual perspective of work.

Boys also look to work to tell them who they are or what their worth is. When a man loses his job, it is a sobering experience. It should be because work is what men do, and we shouldn't enjoy being out of work. However, if our world crashes because we no longer have a particular job, it may be that the job title had become our identity. God doesn't view us as "VP of sales." He views us as his sons.

Boys also judge the value of their job solely on the size of their paycheck. How many times have we been content with how much we made until we heard how much someone else made? Especially, someone we graduated with or see as our equal. We think, *Wait a minute, they're worth more than me?* And it's not always a dollars-and-cents thing. It could be a title or control or relative sexiness of the job.

Just yesterday I learned that Crossroads has been recognized as the fastest growing church in the country. That makes two of the last three years we have received that distinction. Last year we added over six thousand people to our church. We should feel good about ourselves when we accomplish good things, and I would want every man to feel good when a milestone is passed. At the same time, I need to be driven this year to see more people come to our church so that spiritual transformation can take place. Truth be told, I am currently tempted to pull levers just to hit numbers so we can get the recognition three years out of four. If that is what is motivating me, then I'm drifting to boyish ways.

When we look to our jobs to tell us how good we are, we're asking something of work it is not meant to give—our identity. Work is a way we experience God, but it doesn't tell us who we are or what we're worth. The sequence here is important. We are designed to work, but the Bible says we ourselves are God's workmanship—we are a work of God. That's where our value and identity come from. When we get that, we begin to think about our jobs and careers less in terms of a scorecard and more as opportunities to make the best contribution we can based on how God wired us. I know at some level, it's what we all want: work to which we can bring our best, our A-game, our sweet spot, something we're passionate about. That's what God wants for us too.

There's a problem in how we often think about this though. It has to do with a word used in that last paragraph. It's a good word, a healthy word. But it can become a curse if we misunderstand it. The word is *passion*. Warning: I'm getting ready to push against a lot of what's come to be accepted as wisdom. You may not like it. It may smack up against every graduation speech you've heard, every piece of career advice you've received, or every soaring eagle motivational poster in your company's break room. Here it is: finding your passion is *not* the first step to a meaningful career.

What? I thought that was the key. Doesn't the Bible say, "Find a job you love and you'll never have to work a day in your life"? No, it doesn't. I think that was either Confucius or Mark Twain

138

or maybe Ted Nugent. The Bible does, however, say things such as "Whatever you do, work at it with all your heart" (Col. 3:23), and there is a strong theme of serving and working in ways that use our unique gifts and skills. So yes, I'm a big believer in finding a job that makes the most of who we are and where our passions lie. But I think we've gotten the sequence confused.

I'm very thankful that at age fifty-two I'm in a role that both leverages who I am and stretches me. I'm also thankful to be part of several teams with folks who have incredible talents and are working in their sweet spots—musicians, designers, coders, communicators, strategists, carpenters, administrators, you name it. It's a beautiful thing. But I can also tell you that none of them started there. For every one of us, it's been a process of trial and error. And for some of us, it was more error than trial—roles that weren't a good fit, positions we couldn't make work, and jobs that seemed to suck the life out of us. But in each situation we learned and course corrected. Over time, what grew out of those experiences was an understanding not only of what we do and don't do well but also what we are passionate about.

There are some who found their niche at an early age—Bill Gates, Mozart, and Mr. Fischer, my sixth grade teacher, among others. But these are the outliers, maybe 1 percent. For 99 percent of us, passion is something that emerges during a lifetime of work. What God teaches us about ourselves during the trial and error is more important than what we're making. And this learning doesn't end.

One of the saddest sights you'll ever see is the look in the eyes of guys who have stopped learning and growing. Whether in their job or their family or their personal health, they reach a certain stage or milestone and decide they're done. They assume the world will pause along with them. But there is no such thing as a steady state. Whether it has to do with their industry, their wife and family, or their own body, healthy things always grow and move.

I'm no bodybuilder, but weight training will always be a part of my life. Why? It gives a man potential for increased capacity or at least prevents regression. Ride a bicycle, run 10Ks, strength train—but keep moving. No one ever goes into a nursing home because they can't run an eight-minute mile. Often we go into assisted care because we no longer have the strength to maintain our daily activities or to catch our own body's weight when we stumble.

I never got much out of my economics classes in college. (Are you picking up on a trend here with me and college?) They didn't seem to have much to say about the way things really worked. For example, consider the Latin term ceteris paribus, meaning "nothing else changes" or "all other things held equal."[2] In class, they'd describe economic theories and laws that are true about how things work but then say "ceteris paribus"—as long as nothing else changes. The thing is, something *always* changes. There is no such thing as ceteris paribus in life. Things change. And part of being a man of work is that we never stop learning and growing. Some of the guys I know whose lives are having the biggest impact are those who have stayed in the weight room of the trial and error track in their thirties, forties, fifties, and beyond.

I saw an article recently about how algorithms and robotics will at some point in the near future lessen the amount of work we have to do. I don't know exactly when, but looking at the trend, at some point a lot of us are going to be out of a job because a machine will be doing it. Good people have already been put out of work at many checkout lines and factories.

There are obviously huge economic realities to replacing human jobs with robots and algorithms. This will affect our tax code, how people support themselves, and so on. But my first thought was, *Wow, that will wreak spiritual havoc in our culture!* When we get to a place where fewer people can actually produce something and only add value to a robotic economy by consuming, disaster will strike our spiritual and cultural health. Vitality will drop like testosterone in an eighty-year-old man taking estrogen pills. Most people don't think this way because we live in a culture that devalues work.

Men, if you want a life that is in sync with the rhythms God has created, you must learn to value work and to experience God through your work. And you must get a testosterone surge from the very idea of producing value.

18

Boys Act to Serve Themselves.
Men Work to Serve Others.

Recently, the Gallup organization ran a large study to discover how many people actually *work* while at work. They found that 32 percent of people at work are actively engaged, 51 percent are *not* engaged, and 17 percent are *actively disengaged*.[1] This means that almost 70 percent of people are checked out at work. They are intentionally abandoning their call to work. This is a sign of our waning work ethic and disengagement from God.

If your mindset is "I owe, I owe, so off to work I go," you will work like a boy. Some people have hypothesized that the reason Jesus never asked others for money is because he bankrolled his entire ministry from money he saved while working during the first thirty years of his life as a builder. It's conjecture, but it makes a lot of sense, given that we don't see a funding plan through the passing of the plate (or bag if that is your tradition) clearly communicated in the New Testament. Regardless, he worked, whether he was receiving a paycheck or not.

We often toss around the word *vocation* to describe what we do for a living. *Vocation* means a divine call to God's service. It's a function or station in life, and comes from the Latin word *vocare*, which means "to call."[2] We are summoned, or called, to work by God. It's part of how we are wired to bless others. When we work, we serve and bless others. When we don't, we serve only ourselves. In our jobs, we need to consider how we're serving others. If a plumber, we're solving people's problems. If a server in a restaurant, we're helping people enjoy a great meal, and if we're serving dinner to a couple, we're helping to build a marriage.

With some jobs, it may be more difficult to see that labor as altruistically serving. If we're crunching numbers in a cubicle, the person we're serving may be further down the reporting structure or a shareholder. It's important to consider, however, who it is that we're serving in the immediate sense so that we will work with urgency and diligence. Maybe it's the boss, who needs to hit the numbers. Maybe it's a coworker, who is depending on us to deliver a key project. Whoever it is, we need to be serving someone else and not just ourselves.

Jesus said, "The Son of Man came not to be served but to serve, and to give his life as a ransom for many" (Matt. 20:28 ESV). Jesus went to the cross to die for me and you. He came to serve others. Jesus worked! You could easily substitute the word *work* for *serve*: Jesus came not to be worked for but to work.

The picture Jesus gave us is that whatever we do, whether we're a plumber, an investment banker, or a drummer, we're servants first and specialists second. Our work needs to be about serving others. That's not to say we shouldn't be trying to figure out what we uniquely do well and moving toward work that fully engages us. But we do that with a servant mindset.

As I mentioned earlier, my journey has definitely been one of trial and error. When we first launched our church, the idea of homing in on what I did best was a bit of a pipe dream. We were in heavy start-up mode in which the needs were definitely outstripping my capacity as a one-man band. Sermon need to be preached? Check. Room cleaned and set up for a meeting? Check. Unclog the toilet for the nun you're renting office space from? Check. My biggest challenge was hospital visits. If you knew me this wouldn't come as a surprise. I'm not exactly Captain Mercy and Compassion. I think I'm growing in this area, but I'm still more the "suck it up, let's get moving" kind of guy. This works well for a twelve-year-old whining that their feet hurt on a hike but not so much for an eighty-year-old heart patient or a mom who's just had twins.

But start-up mode is a great teacher of servants first and specialists second. It's also how I almost killed one of our board members. Okay, a quick disclaimer: the early years of any start-up are hard. You never get enough sleep, you never have enough resources, and much of what needs to be done is not in your sweet spot. But you do it anyway. Even if you do it poorly, you do it. Disclaimer over.

It started with a phone call. It was early in our church start-up and there were just a few of us on staff. On a Friday morning I got a call that one of our board members, who also happened to be my neighbor, was sick. We'll call him Little Buddy. His real name is Brian Wells, but we'll call him Little Buddy because (1) you won't get confused by the two Brians, (2) I like Gilligan's Island, and (3) it will annoy him. So Little Buddy's wife called and said he was doubled over in pain. They had a baby at the time so she asked if I could take him to the hospital. I was on it. I swung by their house and had him in the emergency room in no time. They ran some tests and diagnosed him as being severely dehydrated from the flu he'd been battling. They put a bunch of tubes in his arm and hooked him up to an IV machine. After monitoring him for a bit, the nurse left to respond to something else. Time went by. He seemed to be doing much better. More time went by. It was just Little Buddy and me in the room. Then the IV machine alarm started flashing and making sounds: beep, beep, beep. It looked like the bag had run out of fluid. Little Buddy was looking better so I figured we were good to go. The system had worked. He was hydrated and the timer was saying "Done."

The alarm kept beeping so I did the perfectly logical thing. I walked around the bed and flipped a few switches on the machine and turned a few dials until the annoying sound stopped. Problem solved. Leader saves the day. I'm no hero, just doing my job. The nurse came rushing back into the room, and for some reason she was not happy. No high five, no thanks for doing my job for me." Instead, she demanded to know who turned the patient's machine off. She started going on about air bubbles and risk of blood clots and other bad-sounding stuff. Who knew? The point is he did just fine. I think we filed that one under "no harm, no foul."

I'm very thankful that my job has morphed over time to one in which I'm focused in on areas of competence. (And I think anyone in our church who goes to the hospital is too.) But we don't start in our sweet spots. Especially, when we're starting out, rather than looking for the perfect job we need to commit to serving others through the job in front of us. There is a beauty and spiritual power in this.

It's telling that, for many, the goal of work is to eventually *not* work. The entire purpose of life and work is to retire? I recognize that there will likely come a time when I won't earn as much money as I do now, and I need to prepare for that, but to spend my whole life saving and preparing for retirement so that I can sit and rot in the sun in Florida while mosquitos suck the blood out of my geriatric skin? No thanks. That is spiritual death.

Think about the older, retired people you know. There are two types of them: those you want to be around and those you don't. The people you want to be around are still working in some capacity. They are serving and creating value. As a result, they are still learning and are interesting to be around because they can carry on a conversation due to new meaningful experiences they are having.

145

Inversely, the people you *don't* want to be around are selfish and miserable. They do whatever they want, and everything is centered around them. They are sixty-five-year-old boys who don't work and can't interact in a vibrant way because they are stagnant spiritually. *There is no way to be spiritually vibrant if we have a bad work ethic because God is a worker.*

At some point, our physical bodies and economic reality will change. But just because we retire doesn't mean that our work must end. My manly father-in-law, Roger, was prepared when he was forced to slow down. He hasn't collected a paycheck in twenty-plus years. This hero of mine recently had a hernia operation, and my wife went to help him out in the hospital. She commented, "Every time I go up to see him, there are nurses just hanging around in the room. Why is that?" You know why? Because when nurses come in, Roger is serving them. He prays for the very people who are serving him. He finds out their kids' and spouses' names. He cleans up after himself as he cleans and stacks hospital plates. He makes life as easy as possible for the hospital staff. He is a worker, even though he doesn't have a paying job. That is what godly work looks like. And that is why I want to be like him when I grow up.

According to a recent study, people who retire at age fifty-five and live to be at least sixty-five have a 37 percent chance of dying sooner than people who retire at age sixty-five. Also, people who retire at fifty-five are 89 percent more likely to die before age sixty-five than those who are still working.[3] If I read this correctly, if we want to die ten years earlier, then retire ten years earlier. We are not wired to disconnect from work!

My youngest daughter recently came to us and said she'd like to take a summer class. We thought, *Who are you?* (That's the last thing I'd wanted to do when I was her age.) We told her that even if she took a class, she'd still have to work over the summer. We said it was important for her personal and spiritual development.

Why was it important? Because we recognized that she needed to *produce* something, even if that meant handing things through the drive-through window at a fast-food restaurant. We are all wired to work, serve, and produce; when we don't, we start to die.

Men work to serve others instead of serving only themselves.

19

Boys Consume.
Men Produce.

When I was a boy in my parents' home, I ate anything and every-thing that was put in front of me. I used and tore every piece of clothing my parents bought for me. I drove and wrecked every car they had. I never thought much about how my dad's job made my consumptive lifestyle possible. I believed it was my right to have and consume anything I could.

That is the way boys operate. They are incapable or unwilling to see the macro plan and spiritual truth of actually producing and adding value. This is why, though I'm no financial expert, I have concerns about the trend I see in our country's economy.

It seems we've moved from being a nation identified by what we produce to a country identified by what we consume. We are more likely to be referred to by the media as American consumers than American citizens.

Maybe one of the first times this became clear was after the 9/11 terrorist attacks. From what I remember of my history classes, when a country went through tough economic times or entered a war, there was a huge push to conserve resources. For instance, when the United States entered WWII, the government and businesses made a big effort to conserve fuel and energy. It was a time of extreme austerity when everything possible was diverted to the war effort. Ration stamps were issued for such things as sugar, cooking oil, and canned goods; once your monthly stamps for an item were used up, you couldn't buy any more. As part of the campaign, a series of billboards was posted along roads that read, "Is this trip necessary?" It was meant not to discourage all driving but to get people to take a more critical look at how they were burning fuel. That's where the term *war time economy* came from. We were a country built on production, and we needed to channel as much of our raw materials and resources as possible to the war effort during that time.

Compare that to what we heard after 9/11. Those in power told us to brace for war, and they had an important message for us: "Keep America rolling!" Keep America rolling? Not conserve? Not produce? No, buy stuff instead. Buy a car, buy a refrigerator, refinance your home. They were terrified that people might spend less. We had to keep this beast moving. Spend, spend, spend. Don't let this fragile house of cards we call the economy topple. Apparently, it is true. When the going gets tough, the tough really do go shopping. (You terrorists can't scare us; we'll show you. We'll buy that new Lexus and HD TV. Take that, Osama!)

Chapters like this would have been helpful for me to read when I had no money. In college I lived with a bunch of guys in a house off campus and blew through my meager monthly meal allotment in the first week. I was often hungry and so poor that I couldn't afford toilet paper.

When Lib and I were first married, we didn't make enough money to buy the double pack of toilet paper to take advantage of the cost savings. I remember standing in the checkout line at the grocer and watching people mindlessly and extravagantly check out with four packs of toilet paper!

Now I can buy the twenty-six pack at Sam's Club for seemingly a penny a roll. This is why it was a good financial move for me to buy a full-size pickup with a six-liter engine. I need the space to haul my cost savings. God bless America!

But as I've aged and my income has climbed, there are new temptations to act like a boy. I can afford to eat out more, but should I? I can afford to buy another gun, but how many are necessary? (I know that none are truly necessary, or at least I hope not, but this is a freedom I enjoy.) However, I can also bring more people to physical and spiritual freedom if I funnel those resources elsewhere. In doing so, I can produce something.

Jesus was put on earth to produce. He created value, he didn't just consume it—even though he was more worthy than others to do so! Anything you want to produce will be tied to some form of work. Want to make more money? Do more work. Want to get a promotion? Work harder. When you work, you produce more value, and you are more of a blessing.

Guys, you do not want to be defined by what you consume. There is nothing wrong with consuming; we all do it. (A lot of us consume way too much, but that's for another chapter.) But, guys, let me say this loud and clear: if you're getting your identity from what you buy—a car, a watch, a cell phone—you are living in the boy zone. One of the reasons I moved away from the Harley brand of motorcycles was because I got turned off by all the Harley memorabilia and clothing. That's why many guys buy Harleys—they want something to match their clothes. Boys identify themselves by what they consume. Men are identified by what they produce.

Everything great that is produced is the result of work. And when you work, "Whatever you do, work heartily, as for the Lord and not as for men, knowing that from the Lord you will receive the inheritance as your reward. You are serving the Lord Christ" (Col. 3:23–24 ESV). Whatever you do, whether repairing a joint on a plumbing line, crunching numbers, building a business, writing a report, managing someone—whatever you do, do it as unto the Lord. Don't slip into autopilot, don't be mindless, don't be disengaged. You are creating something that wouldn't exist if you weren't there. Whatever you do, do it as if God himself is looking over your shoulder. You are serving him.

I acknowledge this is the tougher route. It's much easier to consume, at least in the short term. The producer route is harder. The good stuff usually is. It's like exercise. If you want a laugh, the next time you're in a hotel workout room take a look at the disclaimer sign on the wall. Often, you'll see something like this toward the bottom: "Discontinue use at first sign of discomfort." That, I'm afraid, has become the law of the land for some of us. If taken to heart, that advice would keep me not only off the treadmill and out of the weight room but also away from every difficult job I've ever had, every worthwhile friendship I've ever made, and anything meaningful I've ever produced.

The physiological truth is that until we are uncomfortable lifting a weight, no value is produced. We need the difficulty of micro tears in our muscle fibers to force our body to heal them and build more tissue to support them. This is how we produce muscle, and the discomfort is also why boys don't want to lift in gym class.

If we want to build a business and produce something of value for our families and customers, it will take hard work and even pain for there to be gain.

If we want a relationship to grow, we will have to work at it. We will need to spend time together, converse and open up with each other, and serve each other. It takes work; it doesn't just happen on its own.

If we want a great relationship with God, we will have to work at it. It doesn't simply appear out of the blue. It takes time and effort.

God doesn't ask us to do anything he is not already doing, and God works. Men, if you want to be the man God has wired and called you to be, you need to reclaim the value and importance of work and pour yourself into it each day.

—— —— ——

NOW DO SOMETHING

Read Paul's words about work in Colossians 3:23–24.

Questions to Consider

1. Do you think of work as an inherently good or inherently bad thing? Why?

2. Can you think of a time when your work grew you in a significant way? How did it do this, and how did it change your life or perspective?

3. What work could you do to improve your relationship with someone you care about?

4. Is there something you're avoiding right now because it feels like work, even though you know it's the right thing to do?

5. What act of work do you need to do in the next day to move you toward your vision?

MARK V

MEN ARE PROTECTORS

20

Boys Are Predators.
Men Are Protectors.

What do soldiers do?

Soldiers *protect*. When our country needs them, they step forward from the crowd and say, "I will protect you." They say, "I'll do it whether it's my boots in the mud, my charter in the sea, or my eyes in the sky. I'll go on your behalf. I'll stand shoulder to shoulder with your brother, with your sister. I will laugh with them. I will cry with them. I will fight with them. I will even die with them."

They cut their hair, change their names, take orders, and get up at 4 a.m. and stay up until midnight. They run, they sweat, they push, they haul, they march, they yell, they serve, they beat their chest. They stand in our place. They sacrifice their time and sometimes their lives—lives cut short for you and for me. This is a *soldier*.

What is it that draws men to the military? Though anyone can sign up, only 15 percent of those who do are women. What does that say about men? It says that we are wired and uniquely created to be protectors. Physically, sexually, intellectually, financially, and spiritually, men are protectors.

About thirty miles outside of Cincinnati, there's a sacred space. It's 450 acres of hills that overlook the Ohio River and Kentucky shoreline. It's not sacred because there's a cathedral or monument there. It's sacred because it's the site of Man Camp, a weekend when guys of all stripes, from all over the country gather for two days of man stuff. This includes physical work, play, camping, vices, bonding, worshiping, laughing, and farting. In the process, we exercise physical, relational, emotional, and spiritual muscles we don't often have a chance to. We build real friendships and grow as men. But it's sacred for another reason as well. It's also a land where giants once roamed.

Not far from our Man Camp grounds, the river takes a turn. Before the locks and dams were built, it was one of the narrowest bends of the river. For that reason, during the years before the Civil War it was one of the hottest hot spots for fugitive slave crossings from the slave state of Kentucky to the free state of Ohio.

That's where the giants come in, two men in particular—and I do mean men. John Rankin was a Presbyterian minister who moved his family to a hill above the riverbank in order to be part of the growing slavery resistance movement that would become known as the Underground Railroad. He laid stone steps in the hillside and through the forest 540 feet to his hilltop home where his family, including thirteen children, hung a lantern outside to signal slaves across the river that the coast was clear. Under threat of beatings and death, they defied slaveholders for decades, helping so many fugitive slaves to escape to freedom that "when Henry Ward Beecher was asked at the end of the Civil War, 'Who abolished slavery?,' he answered, 'Reverend John Rankin and his sons did.'"[1]

The other giant was his friend, neighbor, and conspirator in the resistance, John Parker. Parker, himself a former slave, spent years risking his life by sneaking into slave territory and escorting runaways across the river to freedom. At one point, slave owners put a $1,000 bounty on Parker's head. No one knows exactly how many men, women, and children Rankin, Parker, and their teams led to freedom, but it's been estimated to be thousands.

These men were protectors, physical protectors, as all men are—by design.

Generally, men are physically stronger than women. Based on National Strength and Conditioning Association research, men on average are able to produce about one-third more strength and applied force than women, largely due to size of muscle mass.[2] Notice that I said stronger, not tougher. Any man who has witnessed his wife giving birth knows to never, ever compare any pain he might be experiencing to childbirth. I've sawed my finger off with a table saw, totaled my bike riding through a deer's midsection doing 80 without a helmet, and experienced second degree burns on my inner thighs from boiling grease, and I still have no street cred on the pain meter when standing around a group of moms.

When it comes to raw strength, men are wired differently, but I don't think it's just physically. I believe men are also spiritually wired to protect. This may be part of what was going on with young David when he stood up to the giant Goliath. The little shepherd kid wasn't yet the warrior king he would grow into, but it was clearly in him. Or consider Nehemiah, the Old Testament leader who launched the project to rebuild the damaged walls protecting Jerusalem. Nehemiah led a team of everyday citizens, not soldiers, but they were surrounded by people who hated them and wanted to stop them from rebuilding the walls. Nehemiah posted his men along the construction project with swords, spears, and bows with instructions to "fight for your families, your sons and your daughters, your wives and your homes" (Neh. 4:14). That's man stuff right there.

The call for us to protect others against bullies and bad guys of all shapes and sizes is seen throughout the Bible. Men are called to be protectors.

There is one important caveat. This isn't about powering up or flexing muscles or using violence to get what we want. The Bible not only tells us to protect and defend but also warns us, "Do not envy a man of violence and do not choose any of his ways" (Prov. 3:31 ESV). Violence in any form to get our own way is boy stuff. Strength under control used to protect others is man stuff.

Men are protectors, physical protectors. It's in our DNA.

It was in William Wilberforce, a member of British parliament who fought for eighteen years to end the British slave trade and eventually all slavery in the British territories. Wilberforce was a man compelled by his faith to protect those who couldn't defend themselves. He was a man.

It was in Dietrich Bonhoeffer, whose beliefs led him to stand up to Hitler. He was executed in 1945 at Flossenburg concentration camp for his work with the underground resistance. He was a man.

It was in Todd Beamer, the husband, dad, and Oracle account manager who on 9/11 helped lead the group of United 93 passengers against the terrorists who had killed the pilots and commandeered the plane. FBI agents, listening in over the phone, heard Beamer lead the small group in prayer and then utter the words "Let's roll" before storming the cockpit. They gave up their lives but saved unknown destruction to lives and leaders in Washington DC. He was a man.

Men, you can't tell me this is not in you. Maybe between Xboxes and car payments and Netflix marathons, it's been pushed back, but it's in you. We're called to so much more. We're called to protect.

For those of us who are married, it's even clearer. Here is what the apostle Paul says about our job description as husbands: "Husbands, love your wives, just as Christ loved the church and gave himself up for her" (Eph. 5:25). Love my wife as Christ loved the church? So he must mean be nice to her, take care of her, that kind of stuff. But "gave himself up for her" means much more than that. Just as Jesus offered up his life for us, we must be willing to die for our women. There are many good, metaphorical applications here: sacrifice our own needs for hers, give up our money to provide for her and our time to be with her, die in all the little ways that make her feel loved and cared for.

Remember who wrote this passage in Ephesians. This was Paul, whose résumé included imprisoned, flogged, exposed to death, lashed, beaten with rods, stoned, shipwrecked, endangered, sleepless, hungry, thirsty, cold, and naked. I don't think it's a stretch that he's saying men are called to give their lives for their wives, literally, if needed. We're called to be protectors.

The book of 1 Peter shares how a man should relate to his wife. It says: "Likewise, husbands, live with your wives in an understanding way, showing honor to the woman as the weaker vessel, since they are heirs with you of the grace of life, so that your prayers may not be hindered" (1 Pet. 3:7 ESV). It does not say a *lesser* vessel but a *weaker* vessel. I don't know exactly what it means to be a weaker vessel because I know some pretty manly guys who have wives who can do more push-ups than they can. I do know, however, that this means that it is our responsibility as men to do for women what they in many ways can't do for themselves. This happens in big and small ways, but we must always be willing to put ourselves between danger and our families. Your family needs to know that you are their protector.

I have to admit, I've grown up and live in a quite civilized corner of the world. There have been very few times when I've had to physically protect someone who was marginalized or at risk. I do remember one time going into a gym because one of the personal trainers kept flirting with my wife, and it was making me uncomfortable. I put on a puffy sweatshirt so I could take a body blow, went to where he worked out, called him out into the parking lot, and said, "Dude, stop. You can't hit on my wife anymore. This ends now."

It didn't go any further than calling him out (which was a huge relief, honestly). It generally freaks boys out when we call their bluff. But we have to be willing to use our strength to help the marginalized.

We are called to be physical protectors.

21

Boys Want Their Pleasure Today. Men Think about a Woman's Tomorrow.

Can you imagine your reaction if a sixteen-year-old male, a stranger, knocked on your door and expected to borrow your golf clubs? Or your car? We wouldn't give them to him without a detailed explanation of what was going on and what his intentions were. Yet when that same guy comes to pick up our daughter for their first date, we just hand her over. That is crazy. It was not that way with my daughters.

When I was less socially aware, I simply set my shotgun on the kitchen counter when my oldest daughter's first date came to pick her up. It sent a message, but it was incomplete.

The last time this scene unfolded for my youngest daughter, I realized that her potential date was already on his way to pick her up. I said, "He isn't taking you out until I talk with him. You know this is standard operating procedure." When he arrived I said, "Instead of you taking out Moriah, I'm going to take you out. How about you drive?"

While we drove to a local burger joint, I observed whether he was a good driver, which he appeared to be. Then we ordered beverages and I said, "I've known Moriah her whole life, and I love her more than you can imagine. Let's be honest, this relationship isn't likely to last long so I need to ask some questions and get some assurances. First, I need to know that you are going to protect her reputation and only speak well of her both while you are together and when you aren't. Are we clear, and can you do that?"

He said yes.

Then I asked, "What are your sexual intentions? How far do you plan on going?" He answered and I was satisfied. I know that what a young male says in these sorts of conditions doesn't necessarily line up with what he may do when I'm absent and the hormones are raging. Nonetheless, the conversation needed to happen if I was to fulfill my role as a man who protects his family.

What happened when we got home was very telling. Moriah was relieved the meeting was over and had gone well enough for me to release them to carry on with their original plans. Then the texts came in from my older children. One said, "Way to go, Dad." Another said, "Good job in doing the hard work." The whole family had taken notice that Dad was still on point acting as a protector, and everyone took great comfort in that fact. By the way, that young male grew into a man. I'm thankful for the role he has had in my daughter's life.

Statistics indicate that 18–20 percent of all women on college campuses will be either raped or subject to attempted rape.[1] *That's insane!* Why is that? Simple. It's because we have too many boys in our country. They take what isn't theirs for their own pleasure, regardless of the damage.

Nor does this refer only to rape. Boys who would never think of forcing themselves on someone else do think the only rule is whether she's in agreement. "If we're both consenting people, sex is okay." Boys are always like that. They think that if something feels good and they can get away with it, why not do it. If they want to eat a candy bar and no one says they can't, they're going to eat the candy bar.

Single men don't live by the "If I can, I will" code. They actually consider the person they are dating *and* her potential future husband and life. The odds are that whoever you're dating is not likely to become your wife. You need to ask yourself the hard question: "Am I protecting her future, or am I giving her somebody else to compare her future husband against?"

If you do end up marrying her, your sexual self-control now will protect her emotional well-being in the future. A woman knows that a man who controls himself when dating is a man who can control himself with other women later. This will bring incredible peace of mind.

Not only that, you protect your future wife by going into your marriage with as little sexual baggage as possible. I'm not only talking about the possible physical consequences of multiple sex partners. Biblically, there are also spiritual ramifications when a man and woman have sex. You're physically one flesh. Boys are never going to understand that. They don't want to think on a deeper level; they only want what feels good right now.

We live in a culture that pretends the body and the soul can be separated. Often people try to split the body and the soul, sometimes without knowing they are doing it and other times making an intentional decision to violate their conscience or their spiritual beliefs through their physical actions.

My dad did a great job teaching me about sex when I was in grade school. He talked to me about things I hadn't heard of and, frankly, found incredibly weird as a grade-schooler in the 1970s. He checked out books from the library with illustrations. It was very awkward but very helpful in being the first-to-market source for sexual knowledge. In business, the first product in a new category has a competitive advantage over the others. Likewise, if you are first in giving sexual information to your child, it will be more powerful than communication that comes later from others.

But none of that could prepare me for an 8 mm porno reel my friends and I found floating down a creek. I kid you not. Don't tell me there isn't a spiritual enemy in our culture who is trying to mess us up sexually. That movie was an eye-opener and, to a sixth grader, a bit gross. I thought, *Surely my adoptive parents didn't ever do this?!* But they did, and when a husband and wife become one physically, it mirrors the way God is *one* as Father, Son, and Holy Spirit.

This union is a deep, beautiful, and transcendent thing that pornography can never communicate. From my first viewing of that movie at age twelve, the attempt by a spiritual enemy to split my body from my soul was well under way. Those who adhere to this separation tend to fall into two camps. Each thinks they're completely opposite of each other, but in reality, they have a lot in common.

The first group, the sex as appetite camp, says the body and soul can operate independently. They say the soul is spiritual and the body is merely physical so sex is just another appetite. When you feel thirsty, you drink something. When you feel hungry, you eat something. When you feel sexy, you sex something. This is often a favorite philosophy for people who are trying to sell us something. Sex sells. We know there's a power to sex that goes way beyond our ability to explain it. Some of the smartest, most highly paid, and driven people in the world spend long hours trying to understand this mystery and monetize it. Their agenda has been in play for at least a century, and it's been incredibly successful.

When we buy into the "sex is just an appetite to feed" mentality, we think we can share somebody's body without sharing their soul. We look for the buzz of unconditional physical intimacy of two bodies without the unconditional commitment of two souls. But unconditional intimacy with conditional commitment is a tried-and-true cocktail for pain. Or at least emptiness. We want to unconditionally experience someone, physically vulnerable and naked, but we don't want to be vulnerable in any other way. It doesn't work.

Guys, beware: the sex as appetite camp has an impressive history of bringing pain and suffering to otherwise strong warriors, such as King David whom we looked at earlier. David eventually repented before God, and we saw God's amazing capacity for forgiveness. Nonetheless, the remaining years of David's life were a mess, filled with relational tension and governmental complications. There were ramifications that affected his family. In fact, nearly every successive king was more ungodly than the previous one.

But the sex as appetite camp isn't the only one trying to split body and soul. There's also the necessary evil camp. They say the soul is spiritual, and though we need our bodies, they are just inconvenient containers for what really matters, the soul. The body is just a necessary evil. Sex, while necessary, is kind of shameful and dirty, not to be talked about in polite circles. The less we talk about it and the less we think about it, the better.

The necessary evil philosophy is a favorite of a wide variety of religious types and goes back a long way. And I'm not just talking about the nuns in elementary school. Jerome, an early Roman priest from the first century, is recorded as saying, "Anyone who is too passionate a lover with his own wife is himself an adulterer."[2] He went on to imply that the only value of marriage was that it produced virgins. I'm told he never married. What a shocker.

What's interesting is that the necessary evil camp is full of people who say they read the Bible. And by interesting I mean confusing and disturbing. You would think that a quick read through Song of Songs would cure them. It's an erotic love poem between a warrior returning home and his bride. It's so explicit that a lot of church people blush at the very mention of it. I can understand why. It doesn't say "I want to hold your hand." It says, for example, "Your breasts are like two fawns . . . that browse among the lilies" (4:5), "Milk and honey are under your tongue" (4:11), "Come into [my] garden and taste its choice fruit" (4:16). (It also says, "Your hair is like a flock of goats" [4:1], but I wouldn't try that one with the missus.) You get the picture. It's very sexual in nature.

I have a friend whose parents were long-distance dating back in the 1950s. In those days, it meant sending letters back and forth. Whenever his not-yet-married, future mom would receive a letter from his not-yet-married, future dad, all the family, sisters, brothers, mom and dad, and cousins would gather around the dinner table and she would read the letter out loud to them. The future dad would often end his letter with a Bible verse that came to mind when he thought of her for her to look up. One time, fairly early in their dating, his future mom read a letter that ended with the instruction to read Song of Songs 8:7–8. She grabbed the family Bible and read it out loud to the whole family: "Many waters cannot quench love; rivers cannot sweep it away. If one were to give all the wealth of one's house for love, it would be utterly scorned."

It was a very romantic thing to say to your girlfriend, nice and G-rated. Except that's not what she read. Because that's not what he wrote. He meant to write Song of Songs 8:7–8 but got the numbers jumbled. He accidentally wrote Song of Songs 7:7–8. And so my friend's eighteen-year-old future mom cracked open the Bible and proudly read the verses aloud to her gathered family, her large, very conservative 1950s *Leave It to Beaver* family, at the dinner table. "Your stature is like that of the palm, and your breasts like clusters of fruit. I said, 'I will climb the palm tree; I will take hold of its fruit.'"

Whoa there. Strong move, young man. Somehow they recovered and through future correspondence cleared up the mistake and erased the imagery from her little brothers' and sisters' minds. It was their first exposure to the Bible's form of eroticism. I wish that had been my first exposure.

Song of Songs is hot and heavy for a reason. The maker of penises and vaginas is the creator of sex and says there is no splitting of body from soul. It's all one big, beautiful package. It's not just an appetite we feed, and it's not a necessary evil. It's an awesome, mysterious joining of two bodies and two souls that releases power when shared as designed and damages when misused.

Men, we need to reject the toxic sex as appetite and necessary evil camps. It's time to step up and start protecting the women in our lives, and the *future* women in our lives. In the process, we protect our very own selves.

If you are single, define your sexual boundaries before you go out with anyone. And make it a point of conversation on the first date or soon thereafter. You are both thinking about it. Why not bring it into the light in a healthy way? Discover what your biggest sexual temptation points are, draw a line, and take a step back from the line.

If you are married, sit down and make a list of the consequences if you cheat on your wife. The list of things you could potentially lose is long and scary and can serve to protect you and her from future bad choices.

If you are a father, be the first to talk about sex with your kids and do it repeatedly, graphically, and helpfully. Be the first to market with your kids on sex. Don't leave that sacred information to pop culture.

We need to man up sexually. We need to be willing to be different and set a higher standard.

22

Boys Coast.
Men Keep Pushing Themselves.

Sometimes I dream. That he is me.

I dream I move; I dream I groove. Like Mike. If I could be like Mike. . . .

If you're a red-blooded American male between the ages of thirty-five and sixty-five, your heart is pumping right now. If you're younger, you may have no idea what I'm talking about.

"Be like Mike" was a Gatorade commercial in the early 1990s, and Mike was the most incredible athlete of our lifetime. With all due respect to LeBron James, Tom Brady, or whoever else might be on your list, I'm talking about Michael Jordan: six NBA championships, six finals MVP awards, five season MVP awards, ten scoring titles, highest career scoring average in NBA history, highest career scoring play-off average in NBA history, and nine times all-*defensive* team just to start. If the words *Flu Game* or *The Shot* or *Game 6 vs the Jazz* don't mean anything to you, you need to google those right now or turn in your man card.

Back? You're welcome. Now, where were we? Yes, the greatness that was Michael Jordan. Jordan was obviously an incredible, naturally gifted athlete. But he was more than that. Some say his work ethic was even more extreme than his talent. In fact, ESPN's Skip Bayless said Jordan was "the rarest of blends: a supremely talented *over*achiever."[1]

Of course, along with everyone else I was blown away by Jordan's combination of talent, competitiveness, and work ethic. However, looking back at his career there's something that stands out even more—his learning posture. He was a learner. He never stopped learning about the game nor changing *his* game. No matter how great his accomplishments, he kept adding tools to his game.

When he first entered the league, he was known as Air Jordan who could outleap almost anyone on his way to the hoop. Then he added defense to his game and became one of the most ferocious on-the-ball defenders. And just when everyone thought they had him figured out (even though they still couldn't stop him), he added a killer jump shot, including a three-point shot. He also added a slight fadeaway to his shot to create more separation from the defender when he didn't quite have the spring of young legs any longer. Jordan never stopped learning and growing and changing his game. Even after six championship rings, he was a learner. To quote John Wooden, another basketball legend: "It's what you learn after you know it all that counts."[2]

It's a shame but at some point, some guys just stop learning. They decide they're done; they've had enough and want to coast. Boys stagnate intellectually. Not men. Men constantly seek and share knowledge.

After King David died, there were a series of kings who got worse with each generation. One of them was Rehoboam. He came into power and thought, *What can I do to enjoy all the power that I have?* He went to the older men, advisors to the previous king, and asked them what he should do to get the economy going and get people doing the right thing. They advised him to take care of his people and not overwork them. If he took care of the people, they would take care of him, and all would go well. Then the new king sought advice from the younger men, who told him to exert his power and make the people work twice as hard as they had been.

Here's how the book of 1 Kings continues the story: "He abandoned the counsel that the old men gave him and took counsel with the young men who had grown up with him and stood before him" (1 Kings 12:8 ESV). Another way to say this is that he abandoned the counsel of the *men* and took counsel from the *boys* he had grown up with. Likely his thinking went something like this: *Flaunting my power to get my way sounds more exhilarating. I'm better than other people and if I can take from people lower on the "worthiness scale" then that's my right and my pleasure.*

Rehoboam did not lead his people to higher ground. Rather, he drove them harder *into* the ground. He said to the nation: "My father made your yoke heavy, but I will add to your yoke. My father disciplined you with whips, but I will discipline you with scorpions" (v. 14).

Rehoboam fell prey to the classic leader mistake of valuing production over production capacity. He thought he could just say "run faster, rats" without any concern for the health of his people. I have to admit that I have more in common with Rehoboam than I would like to admit. When I set a goal, I push everyone around me. That might be guys I'm leading on a bike trip or people I'm leading on our staff.

For this reason, I'm thankful for Darin Yates being in my life. He is our executive pastor who oversees the operations of our church, including the health of staff. I've met a lot of people in this role who work better with numbers than with people. While Darin is great with numbers, with a master's in Finance from the University of Chicago, he is just as good with people. He doesn't allow his executive function (working with numbers) to overwhelm his pastoral function (working with people). He regularly gives me wisdom related to people, and I'm incredibly grateful.

Rehoboam had that kind of intellectual capital available to him, but he would have none of it. He ignored the wisdom of the older men around him. And as a result, the nation of Israel rebelled and split and was never the same again, simply because a boy refused to receive wisdom from wise men.

Men, this is a huge responsibility. Providing physical protection is real and obviously the need sometimes arises, but it happens rarely. I don't know anyone who has pushed someone out of the way of a speeding car. I don't know anyone who has literally fallen on a grenade or intentionally taken a bullet intended for someone else. But I do know a lot of people who have protected others through the giving and receiving of sound advice at the right time.

We must seek and listen to wisdom from men (not advice from boys), and we must be willing to pass on that wisdom and even challenge others with it when necessary, even if it's unpopular.

Early in the history of Crossroads, when we were growing rapidly and I was regularly being stretched to cope with or do things I had never encountered before, let alone dealt with, I sought out an older man who could give me information I didn't know how to get elsewhere. He was one of the founders of the largest church in the country. He had always wanted to be a professional football coach and he could have been a great one. He coached a flag football team as a volunteer and regularly won championships. People begged to be on his team and under his leadership. His name is Don Cousins, and he went on to raise a son who currently quarterbacks the Minnesota Vikings.

At the time, I was running wild and frying staff members around me. Don said, "You think that you need people to help you get to the goal. You think that if you don't have more people, you can't do what God is asking you to do. More volunteers, more staff, and so on. But remember, it isn't the goal that you need people for. Rather, people *are* the goal. The greatest thing God does is develop people, and that is where you need to focus." Another thirty-year-old couldn't have told me that, but a fifty-year-old was able to see the pattern and give me the coaching I needed.

Men get all the knowledge they can from those who have gone ahead of them. But it doesn't stop there. Men also turn around and share with those who are coming up behind them.

We've done a lot of research at Crossroads on what most contributes to a leader's growth. By far and away, the theme that comes up again and again is the role of mentors. Gaining knowledge and insight from someone ahead of us is the most significant difference maker we've found.

I spend time every week with young entrepreneurs in Cincinnati. They want to be around someone who pushes them in areas their peers can't. They want to hear from a guy who has been married twenty years longer than they have and who has kids twenty years older than theirs.

They aren't the only ones to get something out of our meetings though. Their vibrancy and perspectives help keep me fresh. Being around younger folks in various industries gives me a different perspective on many of the challenges I face. They face similar challenges but take different steps and are having success. Intellectual protection can go from older to younger and from younger to older.

I've never run track, but I'm told that the most important part of a relay race is the exchange. There's a relatively small segment on the track, only twenty meters long, at which the baton can be passed from one runner to the next. You can have the fastest runners in the world, but if you don't nail the exchange, you're out. This is exactly what happened to both the USA men's and women's 4 x 100 relay teams during the qualifying heats at the 2008 Beijing Olympics. Both were medal favorites but they missed the exchange, dropped the baton, and were eliminated. A big part of the crisis of boyhood in our country is due to dropping the baton in the exchange zone.

Men, if you're in your twenties, thirties, or older, you are in the exchange zone. Maybe you are with your dad, who is getting older, maybe with your boss or the owner of your company. There's a relatively small window of time when you can gain knowledge from them and benefit from what they have learned on their lap around the track. Take advantage of this time. Don't waste it. Learn from their lap so yours can be even better.

And start handing off what you know to those coming after you.

Men never stop gaining *and* sharing knowledge.

23

Boys Spend to Zero on Themselves.
Men Achieve Financial Health So They Can Give.

Another realm that a man participates in as a protector is the financial realm.

Money has routinely been an area of tension for me. It is always trying to lure me into boyhood. My parents were very frugal in a healthy way, but to me it felt as though they were squelching the possibility for fun. As soon as I could obtain credit, I rebelled and bought all kinds of things I didn't need and couldn't afford. That put me into a financial prison.

I brought some of those habits into my marriage. It played out as early as our honeymoon, when I took a big portion of our wedding cash and blew it at a casino. My wife had previously dated a coke-sniffing gambler, and my behavior in Puerto Rico made her feel incredibly vulnerable and unsafe.

Lib wasn't much better with money. Our marriage was as much a merger of debt balance sheets as anything else. We had no savings, and we each had car payments and credit card debt. I even had booklets for monthly payments on a television and VCR I had financed. That's right, I took out a loan to buy a VCR. I wasn't exactly a young Warren Buffet.

A few months into our marriage, we realized we were in a pit and needed to take drastic measures in order to get out. We decided to move into my in-laws' house. They're great people, but moving into their attic wasn't on my list of impressive man moves for year one of marriage. At least we didn't have to move into Lib's old bedroom and sleep in her childhood bed. That's where I drew the line. I had to keep some scrap of dignity intact.

We've been married thirty years now, and I'm thrilled to say we made it out of her parents' house. Not only that, we raised, fed, and kept alive three awesome adult kids, helped to pay three college educations, and rode the financial roller coaster all the way. I can say, without exaggeration, we're at the healthiest place financially I could ever imagine.

I'm going to share with you what I learned along the way, but you need to know I'm no financial expert. In fact, I agree with the definition of economics as "common sense made to look difficult."[1] Becoming financially proficient hasn't been easy. But sometimes the best teachers are the ones who have had to fight and grunt their way through it. That's me. So here goes: Money for Men from a recovering financial boy.

The biggest thing I've learned in the last thirty years about how men and boys use money is that *men are givers and boys are getters.* Said another way, *boys spend to zero on themselves; men achieve financial health so they can give.*

Men use finances not only as a way to provide for themselves but also to give protection and help to others. Boys want only to *get* finances to spend on themselves. They don't think about other people. Every dime I earned from my paper route or job as a fast-food worker was consumed by things that had no lasting value. It was boy thinking. I'm not saying it was all bad. I was learning to work and earn and reap the rewards (if you can call thirty-seven dollars after tax a reward. Who is FICA and why does he get half my money?). But thinking of what I could do for others was never on my radar screen.

Fast-forward to a few years after we launched Crossroads. In those early years, the most depressing part of my day was coming out of our rented offices for a lunch meeting, walking down wooden steps to the parking lot, and seeing cars. Those cars represented staff members, and those staff members represented responsibility that was on my shoulders.

I got depressed every time I went out for lunch because when I saw those cars I saw people who were looking to me to protect them financially. I saw people who had left higher-paying jobs to come on staff and I kept thinking, What if I don't do my job well or have some moral failing? What happens then? I realized these fears were in many ways boyish because it was uncomfortable for me to take on financial responsibility for others. I hated the thought. It's still tough for me today, but being able to identify it as a growth area has been helpful. If you're going to be a man, you need to want to be a financial protector. You have to learn to be a financial protector.

That's what God wants for us. In fact, this is such a big thing to God that in the Bible it says anyone who does not provide for their family "has denied the faith and is worse than an unbeliever" (1 Tim. 5:8).

Now that we're clear on how important it is to be a financial protector, I'll share five things I've learned on the way from financial boyhood to manhood. I'm not saying you have to follow these exactly, but I am telling you that these things have worked for me and I'm able to be a protector and blessing to others because of them.

1. Enact a Strategy

Choosing and implementing a strategy may be the most important step. The scary truth is that most of us have no idea where our money goes each month. Or if we do, we think that's just the way it is and there's nothing we can do about it. (Kind of like President Trump's late-night tweets—not good, but what are you going to do about it?) We think money's just going to do what money's going to do.

Money magazine found that one in three Americans have no money saved for retirement.[2] Another way of saying this is that their money tells them where it's going rather than the other way around. When we have no financial strategy, we are like kindergarten soccer players wandering aimlessly around the field. They never score and if they accidentally do, they are as surprised as anyone. Just letting things fall where they may will never put points on the board. To begin, record how you are spending your money every month and then decide if you like what's happening or if you want to change your financial practices.

Some people call money strategies *budgets*. I hate that word. It's boring and comes with a lot of baggage. It makes me think of a constipated bean counter with a spreadsheet and a rule against fun. It doesn't have to be that way.

2. Force the Big Stuff, Forget the Small Stuff

I'm not a guy who could ever live on a detailed budget with everything in their proper columns and monthly allowances: $80 for eating out, $50 for movies, $4.50 for my monthly issue of *Cat Fancy*. (Yes, I have a cat. Men do have cats. It's a proven fact. And just to balance things out I also have a dog the size of a snowmobile, an English Bull Mastiff, so enough with the judging.) Lib and I could never live with that kind of budget. Instead, we've found a method that works for us.

Every once in a while, probably every couple of years or so, we talk about what's important. By *what's important* I mean the big stuff that will matter five years from now, twenty years from now, and when we die. Then we force those payments for those items in our budget. We set them up on automatic withdrawal so we don't have to think about or question them each month. They are things such as giving to our church and other causes, our house payment, our savings, and the like. That's it. The important stuff gets locked in with automatic withdrawals. This is what the IRS does with taxes that come out of our paycheck. We would be well served to follow their example.

The rest of our money goes into a cash envelope from which we take funds during the month for movies, eating out, buying motorcycle parts and camping gear, or whatever we'd like. For years, we used credit cards only for gas purchases. These days we have a little more discipline and financial margin and have relaxed this principle a bit.

There's just one more step we take each month. It's very simple. When the cash is gone, *we stop spending*! Really. If it runs out halfway through the month, the tap is off. This may actually be the part our government could use some work on. They've got the automatic withdrawal part down but apparently are still working on the stop spending part. Still, who are we to say? There aren't many individuals or families that have it nailed either.

3. Contract Paranoidius Upgradius

You may not be familiar with this particular disease, but if you're one of the many millions of Americans who spend more than you make each month, you should be. It's a disease you should be trying to catch. Lib and I caught it years ago, and we don't ever want to be cured. The iPhone gets replaced when it is shattered or runs too slow to even do email. The motorcycle gets replaced when it is wrecked or when a rich guy at a fancy resort in Utah falls in love with my mud-covered manly beast following seven nights on the trail and gives me way more cash on the spot than it's worth.

Here's how the Bible puts it: "Keep your lives free from the love of money and be content with what you have, because God has said, 'Never will I leave you; never will I forsake you'" (Heb. 13:5). There's lots of good stuff there but notice two words, in particular: *free* and *content*.

Contentment might be the biggest secret we've found to financial freedom. One of the things that means for us is we're paranoid about upgrades. We don't buy the latest things. Our cars are never the newest, our phones are usually several numbers behind the latest, and people at Crossroads get sick of me wearing the same clothes on stage. It's not that we never upgrade, but we're very cautious and suspicious when we do. It's a strategic choice and not the default.

4. Embrace Your Thing

Your thing is whatever brings you joy that costs money. You need to budget for it so that it fits within your income and you don't do damage to the big stuff you're forcing yourself to fund. Beyond that, make sure you're strategic about it. Adventure motorcycles, trips, and camping are my thing. Yours might be totally different. Maybe it's knitting. (If that's the case, you might want to put this book down and wait for my wife to write one for you. Just kidding. That's the exact kind of "what is a man" stereotype we don't need any more of. So stop laughing. It's okay to be a man who knits.)

The point is, your thing may not be my thing, but for sure it can't be everything. You have to choose wisely. It's called a strategy (see number one above).

5. Start Now

If number one is the most important step to financial health, this one is a close second. You have to start now. Really. If you do, time is on your side, but only if you start now. Everything in the world is stacked against you: businesses that want your money, banks that want your debt, and unfortunately many of your friends, who live accidental lives and set an unrealistic illusion of endlessly spending. You need to be a man who swims against the current. You need to start now.

You have to figure out how to order your money differently than boys do. You need to find ways to keep your cars running longer or to vacation less expensively so you can have a pool of resources from which to give, save, or do things that boys just aren't interested in. You want to do what it takes to be a financial protector.

A few years ago, I was part of a group of men who met regularly at a diner at the same time every week. One Monday morning, our usual waitress was gone. It was a bit of shock because she was incredibly faithful to her job. We asked what happened to her. Apparently, she was in a difficult place financially. Most of the group had been doing some mix of the five things listed in this chapter for years, and we were grateful to be in a place in which we could do something to help. We talked about it and decided to cover her financially for a couple of months. We just slid cash over the table for her utilities and food. We were being financial protectors. I can't say I've ever felt more like a man than in that moment.

Be a man and prepare yourself for things that may happen in your future, your wife's future, your kids' future, your friend's future, your business's future, your church's future. When you do, you will feel the pleasure of a God who has assigned you the role of protector.

24

Boys Passively Watch Others' Spirituality. Men Proactively Lead Others to True Spirituality.

The final area in which men protect is spirituality.

If you've been to Las Vegas, you probably know who Penn Jillette is, or at least are familiar with his face. His photo is sometimes plastered ten stories high across the front of the Rio Hotel, where he does his magic show. Penn is one half (the talkative, sarcastic half) of Penn & Teller, the longest-running magic act in the history of the Las Vegas strip. Penn, the tall, pony-tailed magician/comedian, is also known for his seasons on *Dancing with the Stars* and *Celebrity Apprentice*—and for his outspoken atheism. He even has cars with the license plates "atheist," "nogod," and "godless." (He said he tried to get the plate "infidel" but wasn't able to for some reason.)

You would think in light of all this, he would be averse to having anyone share their faith with him. You would be wrong. A few years ago, he posted a video sharing his reaction to a fan who approached him after one of his shows and gave him a Bible. Jillette was touched by the man's gift and said:

He was kind, and nice, and sane, and looked me in the eyes, and talked to me, and then gave me this Bible. I've always said I don't respect people who don't proselytize. I don't respect that at all. If you believe there is a heaven and hell, and people could be going to hell or not getting eternal life or whatever, and you think it's not really worth telling them this because it would make it socially awkward, how much do you have to hate somebody to not proselytize? How much do you have to hate someone to believe everlasting life is possible and not tell them that?

He went on to say, "If I believed, beyond a shadow of a doubt, that a truck was coming at you, and you didn't believe it . . . there's a certain point that I tackle you, and this is more important than that."

Jillette closed by saying he was still an atheist but "I'll tell you, he was a very, very, very good man. And that's really important. And with that kind of goodness, it's okay to have that deep of a disagreement. I still think religion does a lot of bad stuff, but, man, that was a good man who gave me that book."[1]

While I don't agree with his conclusion about God, I certainly agree with his conclusion about people of faith. If you truly believe what you believe, how can you not share that with people you care about? I'm not talking about shouting it on a street corner or thumping someone over the head with the Bible at Thanksgiving dinner; I am talking about a respectful conversation with those you care about.

Let's go back to King David. On his deathbed, we see this incredible picture of David spiritually building into his son Solomon:

> And you, Solomon, my son, know the God of your father and serve him with a whole heart and a willing mind, for the LORD searches all hearts and understands every plan and thought. And if you seek him, he will be found by you, but if you forsake him he will cast you off forever. (1 Chron. 28:9 ESV)

This is discipleship. David is chasing after Solomon and developing him all the way to the end of his life.

I hear a lot of dads say things that *sound* enlightened—for example, "I don't want to put my spirituality on my kids. I want to let them figure it out for themselves." That's what a boy says.

Part of the reason many feel this way is because society in general believes that all spiritualties, all ideas, are equal. But they are not. A boy with an undeveloped mind and spirit may think this way. A godly man will not.

It doesn't take much work to see that there are huge differences between the major spiritualties in our world. Some of those differences are so big, there's no way they can all be true. It's intellectual suicide to say that two opposite things are both true. Capitalism and socialism can't both be right. The Atkins diet and vegetarianism can't both produce the same results.

Without getting into a big theological discussion, I'll simply point out that the message of Jesus's sacrifice and our destiny based on grace is radically opposed to every other flavor of spirituality out there. Whether you call it Karma (Hinduism), The Eightfold Path (Buddhism), The Five Pillars of Islam (Islam), or the Law (Judaism), they're all about scorekeeping and working to earn our way. That's called "religion." Some have tried to wrap Jesus's work and mission into a nice bundle of rules, but that's just more religion. What I'm talking about is totally different. It's the clear and simple truth that (1) there is a God, (2) it's not me, (3) we all need grace, and (4) Jesus's sacrifice provides what we need. That's about as far from religion as possible. That's freedom. If that's true, how could you not want your family and your friends to know and experience this sort of transforming power?

Sometimes guys don't engage others in the area of spirituality because they don't want to appear closed minded or judgmental. I'll admit there's been a lot of damage done by people with strong spiritual beliefs—from prejudiced attitudes to shunning those who believe differently to holy wars. We are all in agreement that these kinds of things are wrong and unhealthy.

But here's my question? Is that you? Do *you* think that people who believe differently than you are ignorant or bad or inferior? If so, then keep your mouth shut and ask God to change your heart before you do more damage. If it is not you, then it's critical that your friends and family hear your voice, the voice of someone who can say "I respect you *and* I disagree with you. I am your friend no matter what, but here's what I believe about that." That's a man move.

In his classic book, *Built to Last*, Jim Collins outlines the critical skill that enduring leaders and organizations have of not falling prey to the "tyranny of the or" but instead embracing the "genius of the and."[2] His examples include embracing both stability *and* innovation, predictability *and* chaos, and continuity *and* change. I believe he's right.

The book of John tells us that Jesus came "full of grace and truth" (1:14). These characteristics may seem contradictory, but Jesus brings them together with the "genius of the and." He defines right and wrong *and* he gives freedom in the gray areas. He upholds standards *and* he forgives when they are broken. I was so captivated by this beautiful spiritual matrix that years ago I had my left shoulder tattooed with a design I came up with. It is a modified yin and yang graphic that has grace and truth working together encircled by a crown of thorns. (I felt bad for the tattoo artist who kept bending his needles while trying to puncture my steel-like flesh.)

It is the only tattoo I have on my body because it is the only truth I want to be permanently marked by. (However, I'm very close to getting a YETI cooler tattoo in hopes of them sponsoring me with free product. Maybe this paragraph can count as product placement. Call me!) You can't tell me that the message of grace and truth isn't what your family, friends, teammates, coworkers, city, and our world need. Grace and truth are what men share.

Ever since I was gripped by Jesus's grace and truth in high school, I've consistently kept a list of names on my bathroom mirror. These are people I pray for as I brush my teeth with toothpaste. It is my "paste list" of friends who don't know Jesus's grace and truth. This list has led me to share my faith with a lot of guys, and in the process I've seen many lives radically changed for the better.

The next time the topic of spirituality comes up in the lunchroom or around the watercooler, notice how people who you know have beliefs and convictions clam up and zip it. They zip it because they can't enter a conversation appropriately or don't have the desire to. That's boy stuff. Men say, "Actually, my sense of God is . . ." *and step into the fray.*

A few years ago, my next-door neighbor's tree fell on my house during a storm. (Interesting fact: insurance law says that if your neighbor's tree falls on your house, it's *your* insurance that pays. Nice—for your neighbor, that is.) After we cleared the tree away, my son, Jake, and I made it a project to chop it up and split it for firewood. You've probably seen a tree stump before and know that the rings in the wood grain that circulate out from its core tell you the tree's age. If you look closely though, you'll see that not all of the rings are created equal. Some are thicker and more vibrant. Those were banner years when the tree got just the right amount of sun and rain and underwent great growth. Other rings are thinner and duller. They were years of drought or other extreme weather that stunted its growth.

I'm convinced that if men play the role we're called to play, if we protect spiritually, if we lead others to the same freedom we've found, then years from now, when we're either old and gray or long gone, someone down the line will look at the stumps of our family trees and those we influenced and see big, fat, bold rings. And they'll know that's where change happened, where healing occurred, where truth and love came together. That's where a man was a spiritual protector.

— — —

NOW DO SOMETHING

Read what David's army captain, Joab, said to his brother before going into battle in 2 Samuel 10:12.

Questions to Consider

1. Can you think of a time when you stepped in to protect someone? How about a time when you failed to do so, even though you knew it was the right thing to do?
2. How might you think differently about your finances so that you're able to protect others through them?
3. Can you think of a time when you took an aggressive spiritual stance? Is there a person with whom you need to have a direct spiritual conversation?
4. Are there areas in your life in which you are ignoring the truth because you don't like the ramifications?
5. Are you in some way putting selfish gratification ahead of protecting someone, even if they aren't aware of it?

Conclusion

GET ON IT

My friend Paul is a chiropractor, and he works on my back. He likes to say that he gives me an "adjustment," but that's just a fancy word for a crack. I say, "Hey, man, can you crack my back?"

"No, Brian, it's an adjustment. It's not a crack."

"No, it's a crack, and I need to come into the crack house today."

I can sometimes be stubborn like that in my ideas about things, but often God will unexpectedly and in a heartbeat change my mind. Hebrews says that "the word of God is alive and active. Sharper than any double-edged sword" (Heb. 4:12). This means that when I read the Bible, even if I've read something many times, I could still see it in a way that I hadn't before. I could be dealing with something and I open up the Word of God and suddenly God speaks to me and I say, "Oh, that's exactly what I needed to hear."

Maybe you've had that experience with some of what you've read in this book. Maybe it was exactly what you needed to hear.

That's good, but not great. It's not great until you do something with it.

One of my beefs with our educational system is that it tends to produce people who think that simply because they've read about something or can regurgitate a list of facts, they have grown.

We have a lot of information but don't do anything with it. Some call it the "knowing-doing gap." Until you've actually done something with what you've "learned," no real learning has taken place. One of the things I liked most about my oldest daughter's undergrad experience was that it was a full-on co-op program. She alternated semesters in traditional classroom learning and working full-time in local businesses. Learning has to involve doing.

I'm tired of "awareness campaigns." I'm aware of ALS and it is awful, and I don't want myself or anyone else ever to get it. I'm aware of breast cancer, and it is terrible and needs to be conquered. But guys wearing pink on the football field in the name of making me aware is a tactic that isn't bearing much fruit. We need people funding research and searching for a cure. We don't need to be made more aware of it.

You don't need any more awareness of what a man is. You need to go and be one.

If something you've read here has changed your mind or challenged you to rethink your current state of manhood, that's great. I really am thrilled. But that's not the end. In fact, it's just the beginning.

Have a vision.

Take a minority position.

Be a team player.

Work hard.

Protect those around you.

Epilogue

MAN CAMP

His mother named him Rey, but he will always be Dick Tough
to five hundred other guys in attendance at something we call
Man Camp. Dick Tough's bicep detached from his bone during
an arm wrestling match. That, however, wasn't what earned him
the nickname. He earned his nickname because he stayed in the
match until he lost, reached over to shake the victor's hand with
his wounded arm, and didn't go to the hospital until the next day.
He stayed the night in a tent even though his bicep muscle was
curled up to his shoulder. That's not just tough, that's Dick Tough!

Why would someone in that kind of pain not go immediately to
the hospital? Why would he voluntarily stay and sleep in a bag in a
tent in the woods when he could have been in a bed in a hospital?
To make things worse, that night the temperature dipped to just
below fifteen degrees.

The reason Dick Tough stayed? He didn't want to miss out on
what was happening. The event was too incredible to miss, even
when dealing with a grotesque injury. Amazing! That's the power
of Man Camp.

In the last year, thousands of guys have migrated to the Midwest to get something from Man Camp that civilized culture can't give them: masculine confidence that comes from living out the five marks of a man. Mass media and social media, cubicles, spectator sports, porn, and predictability never bring out the best in a man. They are diversions from the preferred reality that we long for.

Modern society has stolen from us. It has stolen our hardiness by making us dependent on our creature comforts. It has stolen our interdependence on real human beings by giving us pseudoconnections through the internet. It has stolen our ability to problem solve by training us to be victims. It has stolen our ability to commune with God in silence by continually dangling some shiny new object in front of our faces, some winsome piece of media that is initially attractive but ultimately disappointing.

As a result, a man loses his competence in the skills and the "get it done" attitude that the ancient fraternal order of men has mastered since the beginning of time. These are the things that Man Camp instills in a concentrated period of time.

Most guys haven't worked hard, labored outdoors, played physical games, hiked a mile with forty pounds on their backs, sung loudly in public, received prayer while other men touched them, spent an hour in solitude, heard talks that spoke to their souls, told other guys their struggles, had more than one beer, been baptized in freezing cold water, or slept on the ground outside a temperature-controlled environment in a very long time—if ever.

This entire experiment started when I took my seventeen-year-old son out West for his manhood initiation. My idea of roughing it used to be staying at a Motel 6 without Wi-Fi and Starbucks, but that all changed on this trip. We rode a giant loop that caught the Grand Canyon on the southernmost tip and Glacier National Park to the north. Feeding two guys, gassing two bikes, and staying in hotels for ten days would have been a financial drain. So we camped along the way with friends. Somewhere in the process

I fell in love with the adventure, uncertainty, and mellowness of sitting around a campfire, sleeping under the stars, and pooping in the great outdoors as God intended.

In the years that followed, we formed a tight community that rides endless paved twists and dirt roads from the Rocky Mountains to the Canadian Rockies to Alaska, though most of the time it's just weekend trips through the hills and streams of Kentucky. I've been averaging thirty nights of camping a year for the past five years.

Man Camp was born out of a campfire conversation on one of these trips. We were recovering from a difficult day of rain and broken bikes. It dawned on us that the hardships and problem solving forced on us that day, and the resulting confidence we felt, were things most of us didn't get in our day jobs. Overcoming difficulty together is like glue for deep male friendships. And it was forcing us to deal head-on with the presence or the lack of the five marks of a man in our lives.

As we discussed this, our only regret was that some brothers couldn't share in that moment around the fire. Not everyone wants to ride a bike or can afford a bike and the necessary gear. Fortunately (or unfortunately), adventure riding isn't one of the marks of being a man. But we wanted to make the things we experienced more accessible to a lot more men. That's when the idea for Man Camp was born.

I can't tell you a lot about what happens in the forty-four hours of a typical Man Camp, because within the first hour we commit that "what happens at Man Camp stays at Man Camp." What I can tell you is that thousands of men laugh like they haven't since high school, play like they haven't since grade school, work and use their muscles as they were designed to be used, pray like they didn't think they were qualified to pray, and maybe most importantly open up to each other in ways that just don't happen in normal day-to-day life. I've attended dozens of conferences and hundreds of training sessions in my life, and I've never seen men come alive as I have in two days spent out of their comfort zone focused on the five marks.

Our culture has stolen something from us, and Man Camp seeks to reawaken the male who was designed by God to be a man. Thousands of women saw a boy leave for the weekend and a man return. One such man is Jason. Following is his story in his own words:

Coming into Man Camp, I thought this was going to simply be another camping trip. We would roast some hotdogs on the campfire, get cold in a sleeping bag, and come home. But it was so much more than that. The first thing I noticed was in our first gathering—all 500 men singing. You don't expect men to want to sing in front of other men, but there was a sense we were all in this together and we all wanted more out of life. I found myself singing louder and with more conviction than I ever had in church. The next thing that moved me was working with 500 other men to clear dead trees, brush, and trash off the land that we were blessed to have as a campsite. We celebrated and high-fived each other like we won the Super Bowl, doing really hard work and getting our hands dirty as a team.

What happened later that night around the campfire was the turning point. As men often do around a fire, we shared some beers, insults, and funny stories. But then the men in my group began to let down their guard and talk about their vision for the future. It got to me. I don't speak very well in groups. I'm almost 40. My wife and I have two blessings in our children and we both have great jobs. But something came over me to tell my group about how I want to become a better person, a better husband to my wife—I talk down to her, I lie about things, and even though I LOVE her, I don't show it; a better father to my children—I have a short temper with them and in general don't spend time building into them; and a better man. I don't hang out with the right group of men doing the right things. I don't pray and give thanks to God for all that he has given me. I realize I can no longer act godly only when it is convenient. I cried, we cried, and leaders in my group prayed for me. It was the first time a group of men put their hands on me and prayed for me. My face was so wet from tears.

The next thing I did was lay it all out there with my group. First, I'm disgusted in one thing that I took with me on this trip, a vice of mine, weed. I grabbed my vice and threw it into the fire. My group was so great. We prayed together again. I have told my wife I would stop this vice over and over again, so much that she doesn't trust me anymore. I threw my vice into the fire right then and there, so that my group would hold me accountable. I believe this vice is what is holding me back from being a better husband, father, and man. I now have taken the first step in becoming a better person. I know I have a lot further to go.

But what happened next was even better. I got home!!! The first thing I did was rush over to my wife and give her the biggest hug I have ever given her (probably the first one I really meant too). I told her I love her. I told her I want to be a better husband, father, and man. I told her about the vice I took with me; she was disappointed and probably not surprised that I took it. I told her about putting it in the fire. She heard me, but isn't convinced I'm done. It's now time for me to execute. My little one ran over to me. I picked her up and hugged her for a long time and told her I loved her and wanted to be a better daddy to her. Later, she kept on telling me she loved me. This camping trip was just what my life needed, it's what my family needed, and it's what my relationship with God needed. Thank you . . . Thank you . . . Thank you!!!

Man Camp is for males ages eighteen and over who need something different. It's for men who want to experience practical application of the five marks of a man in a rigorous environment. The vast majority of men who have attended Man Camp are not experienced campers. Many have never spent a single night in a tent. That's not what matters. What matters is that every man who attends Man Camp wants something different. They see the damage the world can do to men, and they take ownership of taking their life in a different direction.

We would love for you to join us at a future Man Camp. If you are interested, visit us at briantome.com.

Notes

Introduction

1. Research results on the effect of absent fathers was compiled by the National Fatherhood Initiative, http://www.fatherhood.org/father-absence-statistics.

2. Matthew Gault, "Sebastian Junger Knows Why Young Men Go to War: The Filmmaker Discusses Combat and America's Male Identity Crisis," War Is Boring, January 28, 2015, https://medium.com/war-is-boring/sebastian-junger -knows-why-young-men-go-to-war-f163804cbf6.

3. John Foxe, *Foxe's Book of Martyrs* (England: John Day, 1563), http://www .exclassics.com/foxe/foxe323.htm.

Chapter 1 Boys Are Shortsighted. Men Play the Long Game.

1. Jason Snell, "Steve Jobs: Making a Dent in the Universe," Macworld, October 6, 2011, https://www.macworld.com/article/1162827/macs/steve-jobs-making-a -dent-in-the-universe.html.

Chapter 2 Boys Live for Today. Men Think Long Term.

1. Stephen Mansfield, *The Search for God and Guinness: A Biography of the Beer That Changed the World* (Nashville: Thomas Nelson, 2014).

Chapter 3 Boys Drift. Men Focus.

1. Brandon Griggs, "10 Great Quotes from Steve Jobs," CNN, updated January 4, 2016, https://www.cnn.com/2012/10/04/tech/innovation/steve-jobs-quotes /index.html.

2. Gordon MacDonald, *Ordering Your Private World* (Nashville: Thomas Nelson, 2003).

Chapter 5 Boys Want to Go with the Flow. Men Are Willing to Stand against the Tide.

1. Peter McAllister, *Manthropology* (New York: St. Martin's Press, 2009).

Chapter 6 Boys Want to Fit In. Men Aren't Afraid to Stand Out.

1. Wikipedia, s.v. "August Landmesser," last modified February 24, 2018, https://en.wikipedia.org/wiki/August_Landmesser.

Chaper 7 Boys Are Fractions. Men Are Whole.

1. See "Sidenote #1: Why Vice Is Considered Manly," in Brett McKay, "Where Does Manhood Come From?," *The Art of Manliness* (podcast), April 21, 2014, https://www.artofmanliness.com/2014/04/21/where-does-manhood-come-from/.

Chapter 9 Boys Are Lone Wolves. Men Run in Packs.

1. "Suicide: Facts at a Glance," Centers for Disease Control, 2015, http://www.cdc.gov/violenceprevention/pdf/suicide-datasheet-a.pdf.
2. Dean Ornish, *Love and Survival: The Scientific Basis for the Healing Power of Intimacy* (New York: HarperCollins, 1998), 2–3.

Chapter 10 Boys Are Passive. Men Are Active.

1. John Gray, *Men Are from Mars, Women Are from Venus* (New York: HarperCollins, 1992), chap. 3.
2. Sebastian Junger, *Tribe: On Homecoming and Belonging* (New York: Hachette Book Group, 2016).
3. Sebastian Junger, "Why Veterans Miss War," TEDSalon, January 2014, 8:16, https://www.ted.com/talks/sebastian_junger_why_veterans_miss_war.
4. C. S. Lewis, *The Four Loves* (New York: Harper Collins, 1960), 71.
5. Jon E. Grant and Marc N. Potenza, eds., *Young Adult Mental Health* (New York: Oxford University Press, 2010), 97.

Chapter 11 Boys Reject Authority. Men Respect Authority.

1. "The Delinquent: A Spate of Rhino Killings," *CBS News*, August 22, 2000, https://www.cbsnews.com/news/the-delinquents/.
2. English Oxford Dictionaries, s.v. "rebuke," https://en.oxforddictionaries.com/definition/rebuke.
3. G. K. Chesterton, *Collected Works*, vol. 28 (San Francisco: Ignatius Press, 1987); see Dale Ahlquist, "Lecture 91: The Boat on a Stormy Sea," American Chesterton Society, accessed April 18, 2018, https://www.chesterton.org/lecture-91/.

Chapter 14 Boys Tear Each Other Down. Men Build Each Other Up.

1. Louis Cozolino, *The Social Neuroscience of Education: Optimizing Attachment and Learning in the Classroom* (New York: W. W. Norton, 2013).

Chapter 15 Boys Live to Play. Men Play to Live.

1. "US 14th Happiest Country in the World," The Daily Journalist, April 16, 2018, http://thedailyjournalist.com/scientia/us-14th-happiest-country-in-the-world/.

2. Stuart Brown, "Personal Health and Well Being," National Institute for Play, accessed April 18, 2018, http://www.nifplay.org/opportunities/personal-health/.

3. "Discovering the Importance of Play through Personal Histories and Brain Images: An interview with Stuart L. Brown," *American Journal of Play* (Spring 2009), 399–412, http://www.journalofplay.org/sites/www.journalofplay.org/files /pdf-articles/1-4-interview-importance-of-play-stuart-brown.pdf.

Chaper 17 Boys Work to Stake Claims. Men Work to Experience God.

1. Henry Blackaby and Claude King, *Experiencing God: Knowing and Doing the Will of God* (Nashville: LifeWay, 1990).

2. Wikipedia, s.v. "ceteris paribus," https://en.wikipedia.org/wiki/Ceteris_par ibus.

Chapter 18 Boys Act to Serve Themselves. Men Work to Serve Others.

1. Amy Adkins, "Employee Engagement in U.S. Stagnant in 2015," Gallup, January 13, 2016, http://www.gallup.com/poll/188144/employee-engagement -stagnant-2015.aspx.

2. Wiktionary, s.v. "vocare," https://en.wiktionary.org/wiki/vocare.

3. "Early Retirees May Face Earlier Death, Study Finds," Fox News, October 21, 2005, http://www.foxnews.com/story/2005/10/21/early-retirees-may-face-earlier -death-study-finds.html.

Chapter 20 Boys Are Predators. Men Are Protectors.

1. Wikipedia, s.v. "John Rankin (abolitionist)," accessed April 18, 2018, https:// en.wikipedia.org/wiki/John_Rankin_(abolitionist).

2. Terry, Williams, "Muscular Strength in Women Compared to Men," September 11, 2017, Live Strong, https://www.livestrong.com/article/509536-muscular -strength-in-women-compared-to-men/.

Chapter 21 Boys Want Their Pleasure Today. Men Think about a Woman's Tomorrow.

1. Abby Ohlheiser, "Study Finds 'Epidemic of Sexual Assault among First-Year Women at One U.S. College," *Washington Post*, May 20, 2015, https://www .washingtonpost.com/news/grade-point/wp/2015/05/20/study-finds-epidemic-of -sexual-assault-among-first-year-women-at-one-u-s-college/.

2. "Reinventing Family Life," Christian History Institute, accessed April 11, 2018, https://christianhistoryinstitute.org/magazine/article/reinventing-family-life.

Chapter 22 Boys Coast. Men Keep Pushing Themselves.

1. Skip Bayless, "Just Be Thankful for Jordan," *Chicago Tribune*, May 16, 1998, emphasis added, http://articles.chicagotribune.com/1998-05-16/sports/98 05160020_1_bulls-organization-reggie-miller-jerry-krause.

2. Ben Hanback, "What Will You Learn after You Know It All?," *Tennessean*, January 3, 2016, https://www.tennessean.com/story/money/2016/01/03/what-you -learn-after-you-know-all/78108188/.

Chapter 23 Boys Spend to Zero on Themselves. Men Achieve Financial Health So They Can Give.

1. Ha-Joon Chang, *Economics: The User's Guide* (New York: Bloomsbury Press, 2014), 3.

2. Elyssa Kirkham, "1 in 3 Americans Has Saved $0 for Retirement," *Money*, March 14, 2016, http://time.com/money/4258451/retirement-savings-survey/.

Chapter 24 Boys Passively Watch Others' Spirituality. Men Proactively Lead Others to True Spirituality.

1. Penn Jillette, "A Gift of a Bible," YouTube video, 5:11, posted by "beinzee," July 8, 2010, https://www.youtube.com/watch?v=6md638smQd8.

2. Jim Collins and Jerry Porras, *Built to Last: Successful Habits of Visionary Companies* (New York: HarperCollins, 1994).

Brian Tome is the founding and senior pastor of Crossroads, a multisite church in Cincinnati, Ohio. Crossroads started in 1995 with eleven people, and has since grown to over thirty thousand people in twelve sites across the country. Brian is passionate about feeding and educating children in Nicaragua, empowering entrepreneurs, supporting women and girls rescued from sex slavery in India, and adventure motorcycle riding. He has authored two other books, *Welcome to the Revolution* and *Free Book*. He and his wife, Libby, have three children and reside in Cincinnati.

CONNECT WITH **BRIAN TOME** ONLINE AT

BRIANTOME.COM

• • • • •

 @BrianTome @BrianDTome  @BrianTome @BriTome